TIME BETWEEN

Paul Williams & Family

"Loneliness is the sole motivation, &
the only pain I feel is all this
time between
you and me . . ."
—Mel Lyman, Chris Hillman

Entwhistle Books

Cover photo by Carolanne Currier: Paul Williams at Galley Bay, July 1970,
during the writing of *Das Energi* and five months after the last page of *Time Between*

Cover logo by Bhob Stewart

Digital remastering by Jeff Schalles

this book available from:
Entwhistle Books
Box 232517
Encinitas CA 92023 USA

and from: www.paulwilliams.com

or: 760-753-1815

Portions of this book have appeared in *Fusion* and *The Green Mountain Post*

Thanks to David Hartwell and Audrey Sabol for their help in first publishing this
book; and thanks to Tom and Judy Brown, Lark Clark, Carolanne Currier, Alan
Graham and Peter Gould for their help in writing the book. Thanks to Wally Conger
for the use of his 1973 review on the back cover of this edition.

this book is for Miriam knight
and Alan Graham

Where am I? Do you want a time or space answer?

No.

I'm on the first page of a full report/
      in the middle of the Rolling Stones Jefferson Airplan
            Bob Crumb Lark
         my room
               & Carolanne's
         talkin' bout the midnight rambler
            everybody got to go

December 27 1969 Mendocino
               I want to tell you everything.

     I got the idea for this on water, on the Casino Pool 28-foot
sailboat skipper Ian Corrance somewhere west of Cortes Island and
heading south. I was in the middle of Allen Ginsberg being interviewed
in Playboy pages wet and peeling Ginsberg so clear I felt: jealous?
no not quite but moved to be far more myself to really get it out
say it clear and now no more messing around very high energy emotion
bursting slightly mad and I conceived the idea of writing a full report, trapped on a typewriter with Rolling Stones Airplane coming
through my ears sooner or later everything going outmy fingers clear
it all out going out of business sale everybody got to

     go: Alan failed to stop for a red light strung among the Xmas
decorations in Powell River now he refuses to drive
                                        gasoline vehicles
inhale life spit death
                  get you there
                         ^   the hell with that. Break on

          thru

second page "Little Saint Nick" The Beach Boys Christmas album
Lark is Christmas over "oh no" okay
Spain & Crumb off to call Bob's wife
  "Do I scare Carolanne?"
                              "No I don't think so. I don't."
Al Jardine has nice legs/Lark would have been hung up on him in hi
                                                          school

   strange to write as it happens. especially dialogue. does that
mean this is reality?
                     Whose?

Not meaning to ask a lot of questions; this is mostly to tell you
stuff. I want to purge my mind of things you might want to know
or think about
               substitute for "you" I
   "Sometimes I think I'd like to start over again as a virgin
    in another town" (Playboy cartoon girl)
                                   clean slate/fresh start
since we've phased out guilt now all there is to get rid of is garbage

   Here it comes:

                  (Tommy now playing) I was born in humble Boston Mass
in March I am going to build a log cabin
                                    and have a kid
   (Yarrow born February 12th now ten months old)
      this is time between

 When I was eighteen (only a few days) I first made love
to Angela, who wasn't too happy about it
  and walked down Cambridge streets later thinking "Huh. I did it!
Am I different now? Do I feel different? Was it really all that much
fun? Well, it was nice. Yeah but not really exciting...?" (I only
hinted at this last, in my thoughts; to doubt the excitement of Doing
It seemed sacrilege. And it was all not quite real yet, anyway.)

Perhaps a year later I began to unself-consciously enjoy sex.

And   thought I was slow; but it seems I was faster than most.

    Tommy is difficult to write to; I want to scream orders. What?
Neo-fascist tendencies? Oh, good gracious!
                         Well, don't worry; I don't
like the sound of orders
                   screamed or not.

   I'm 4F (psychotic). And I'm going to Canada.

Where is Carolanne? Where is everybody? I could stop writing and
go take a look... But the idea was, stay at the typewriter (sneak-
ing off occasionally to the woods and the kitchen). I don't want
to. I'm lonely. Bored. Self-discipline. This is silly. Already
I feel pressure building up, tension: this is supposedly good for
my art. Conflict. Duality. Here as not-There. Damn it!

Whichever girl comes back first I'll make love to.

   No, I can't stick to that. Too scary. I mean, you have to consider timing, appropriateness, fairness to all, fear of rejection,
um... I just don't want to make my decisions by fiat. Even for the
sake of throwing changes. Change happens fast enough all by itself.
Well no, that's not always true. Maybe I am always engaged in de-
liberate efforts to _cause_ change. Not always: half the time. The
other half receptive, let it happen. Let it be/let it bleed::receptive/
creative Beatles and Stones as complements, opposites... who cares?
  "Come on now baby, don't you want (All You Need Is Love/We Love You)
   to live with me?"
                    so far no music this page.

      I love you.   That's music.   says Carolanne, who, it turns
out, also has access to the typewriter. Which changes things. Everything changes. I did go into the other house, found Lark Carol Bob
Kay Spain in Phyllis' old room, Lark's room, Aeko there also but
quiet, sleeping, tossing a bit, warm comfortable room with candles
and one efctric light, Lark up on tne bed built high beneath the
window like mine, you can look out, jump out, jump in maybe, it
makes the room bigger, two levels, bed and floor. Why don't we do
it in the road. Memory of Trina and I on the floor on East 4th,
we sure had fun. Lark, Spain, Bob all from Trina reality here in
mine, but Lark also through Don and part of me depuis longtemps as
well. And Kay & Ron good friends of Bob too, as well as Lark, in
fact Bob L, also visiting, almost got Bob C to move in downstairs
of him. Confluence. Happens every day. I wrote about Bob (Head Comix)
more than a year ago, and tonight he read what I wrote.

      I like him. A funny, honest, real-seeming person. Lives an hour
and a half east of here, and after just-missing twice in Haight St.
head shop   1967 we finally get together, my karass closing in but
Do I feel different?
                    Yeah maybe. Constant change.

I don't want to just play around. There's plenty in my head, visions,
awareness, explanations, adventures, desires, lists of things to say
and do and now my chance, act out all lists say it say it don't hold
back do it if you are sincere you have success in your heart
            and whatever you do succeeds

                  the abysmal repeated

      can I bridge this distance?

I'm afraid of boring you. If I get involved enough, mad enough,
it'll all pour out so fast and furry and schizophrenic you'll have
to slow down to read me, better than wanting to speed up because
I'm not saying enough fast enough, is this introduction necessary
do I have to build up to something or can I just wait till I'm crazy
and then start spitting words? We do not communicate our whole selves
because only when we're in certain moods & frames of mind do we have
the desire to communicate; a lot of states of consciousness are
therefore left out. There are things I don't talk to anyone abuut,
I think, and certainly things I say to one person that never come
up in conversation with another, and what appears in my books is
different stuff again, the speaker/writer is only half the communication, the audience, immediate or eventual, is the other half,
the other whole I should say, two simultaneous wholes make up one
dynamic reality, these words would mean nothing if they were falling
in the forest with no one around to eat them.

    I would never have given Andy & Judy acid if I'd thought
they were going to take it in the city!

    LSD slowly coming on--Jefferson Airplane "Eskimo Blue Day"
    Al visiting--another Altamont veteran. So many of us have been
through the same baths! Good morning--cleaned out the woodshed
of dogshit & garbage, loaded truck for a dump run, more wood to
woodshed by wheelbarrow (no more inessential use of truck), sawhorse
set up and a growing pile of firewood cut by swedesaw... much more
satisfying, hedonic than speed-mad chainsaw (possibly the right
tool for certain jobs--must be used maturely, patiently--wish it
didn't burn gasoline...).
    Al is reading Tim Leary interview in the
Barb, talks about Altamont, Woodstock, running for governor etc--
Tim almost the only good news in the whole paper, god he's really
doing a fine service. I'm disgusted that Max is still running those
ugly ads... he's learned nothing. Money's a hard master even for
"revolutionaries" to break free of. Perhaps certain individuals
should be tarred & feathered with honey and dollar bills. Oh well.
Pray for a depression.

    Nice cereal Kay made, sorry I snapped at her--I don't want
to eat much, don't want to see stuff wasted either... she was just
responding to my plaint that all the pancakes were eaten while I
was out working... truth is I probably wanted to bitch more than
I wanted to eat.
    We trap ourselves in our excess energy.

    Alan vs. Tami in the background, laughter & tears and the
Yellow Kid to the rescue. Tami cries for what she wants, Alan laughs
in defense. Each of us is most of the time ourself, what more can
we expect of us? Tears painful to me in the foreground, more so than
Raven crying who I know cries for more and who I respond to when I
can but Tami though she may not cry as much is harder to please: more
mature, more defenses. Raven screams openly; that's her nature. Her
mother screaming likewise seems more than we can take. Different context?

Tami: "Why can't he get angry at other people besides me?"
     good question. Maybe because he makes love only to you

     Al in his Woodstock jacket is a flash. And I'm getting high.
But (an hour later) not as high as I'd wanted. 1 mean, 1'm not
confused.
          This reality is getting so good the lsd doesn't distort
it at all.
          (took the burro for a walk) I'm going to consult the
I Ching.

     small dogs in the house

               abundance/the marrying maiden, which suggests to me
that taking more acid in an effort to become more satisfyingly confused would be unwise. This is the first time I've used my yarrowstalks. Lark gave them to me Christmas--very special magic, yarrow
from Roots, the place Don and Trina and I had in the country... okay,
some exposition:
               (Carolanne listening to Honky Tonk Women on headphones)
Don McNeill   oh Don
    born winter solstice 1944   my close friend of acid trips & music
   New York City and Monroe   shared lifetime spring 67 thru summer 68
          drowned in the lake of an evening swim Roots August '68
     I was in Boston that weekend/Trina had just aborted our child/Clinton
Carter, my closest friend from age 6 to well into high school had died
mysteriously on the west coast/the trip to Boston was to buy a Volkswagen
bus, in which Don and I would drive to Alaska/at last escaping New York
and going to The Country/or some unknown adventure/as I mourned Clinton
and prepared escape from vanished child and love affair/I had found a
good bus/Don went under
               (Carolanne Canned Heat)
     and Lark dear sexy sagittarius my first lover during Trina
     Don wanted to marry her once he may have died a virgin
          she and Steve, Kim and Trina staying at Roots, still a place
in the country for folks stuck in the city
                              Lark picked yarrow
     summer 69   and dried the stalks and thought of me
          and now she's here
                              to give me sticks with Don and Trina in them
Don and Trina and Lark and me, special magic stalks
          pain, love & time
                    abundance

(notes in pentel from last night)

          I want to affirm reality.
     This stuff is all spontaneous--if nothing happens, I'll
throw it away. But something will happen...
          I'll make it happen
               The Creative: demon-artist
               earth-mover   star-dweller
                    I will free myself
                 from bland existence
                      and dance exquisite fantasy on printed page

--no, that's bullshit; it's my art that's boring
  my life is the most fascinating I've ever had
lots of pretty girls, babies, trees, meaningful work &
 loving friends, good music gourmet (organic) food...
          stuff happening all the time
          loving Carolanne to lie in bed with
            Tom and the free school, Alan and the ocean
            and enthusiasm galore
                         British Columbia
new frontiers! We shall all be sailors, farmers, divers,
lovers, carpenters... mountain ocean forest dwellers
                we shall all be all
     we are already heroes beyond our wildest dreams
   yesterday's fantasies are of yesterday's fabric
    today's visions are truthful now!
                              dynamic
                                   energy

work with your energy, ride it, herd it

   the economics of energy is the science of awareness

   we are the world and we want it

          & female receptive earth's responsive
               to male heaven fucking touch
                  creative allness who is God is man
                  is all life, things that breathe
               and sweat and cycle through the Ecosystem

     I am
          self-awareness that you and the redwood share
     consciousness

               I am earthman! I am God! I am life
                              incarnate

I am a single disposable cell and I am the entire unit
        the whole fucking thing
            I can do anything
        big deal
    so why are you (why am I(here) mutilating myself?

        I forgot he was me.

    Dear Paul You make me feel good I'm trying to do what I
want mostly it's hard & only those moments of break through
or maybe it's those moments of ecstasy I'm where I belong
for the first time in my life how long can it last. Or perhaps
this is just the beginning? Can I grow? Now that I've established
the love between me & the people here or that I do love myself,
where do we go from here. I'm left looking at myself, beautiful
but so what as I said to Crumb as we hiked the Appalachian
Trail, beautiful but so what? Oh Lark he said & kissed me. I
love you Paul/but I need your
help.
                                        (Lark)

    Now Raven will help us. I've moved the typewriter and its
table outdoors into the sun (extension cord) and I have Raven in
one hand, typing with one finger of the other. She's been in a
jolly mood for days. Lark is leaning over me I like it listening
to Otis Redding who she really digs Aeko calls to us from indoors
Aeko a Taurus born May 7
                I'll Let Nothing Seperate Us--Otis Redding song
that got Lark across the country
                        to Bob--she had the idea the country
was between them (New York/ /California) so she thought of the song
        for strength for energy
                    break on through
                                    she made it
    Raven an Aries April 19
                    mad Mel Lyman demanding the world and she
wants it   wow! is she happy today
                            in Carolanne's hands she whirls
    and spins   in her crib she grabs the side (it's up to her waist),
grinning, jumping jolly enthusiasm and Lark sure is into Otis
    "I don't know what you're allowed to wish for"   she says she
still loves Bob tho all including me have told her not to; I say, that's
not what I think I told you... I said don't count on anything. But
you know it's always a good idea to love... I didn't make myself clear
before. Maybe I'm doing it now?
                    There is only now.

closer to reality

     I Paul Williams have written many books
                             in my mind:

 Breakaway is about our move to British Columbia and an attempt
to put in words our general need to remove ourselves completely
from dependence on the old social economic political forms and
the institutions, codes, concepts and assumptions those forms spawned.
Break away. Different image than drop out, because times change and
it's years and centuries later now--we need not go "out" but "away."
And having broken away, you discover your own center, no more worlds
we never made when we can make our own whenever we feel like it.

Gathering Together is a collection of stuff, somehow about the massing
of energy, the desire of people and ideas and actions to get together,
somehow a book about a period of my life whose most exalted state is/
has been that described in the I Ching hexagram the title is taken from.
The book includes my Woodstock report, the conversation between Tim &
Rosemary, John & Yoko and me,   various other letters and essays,
songs and poems that have come out of me since Pushing Upward was com-
pleted, stuff... stuff is clay, ether, whatever's around when you want
to create something.

Fortune Teller: my "novel," ultimate book, exists only as telepathic
moments of superconscious delight confusion of identity "reader" "protagonist" "author" all become one and thence any of the three, story
of the present through future and past, post-Babel literature no longer
distinguishable from love thiotimoline melange Rolling Stones: Now I'm
a fortunate feller/Married to the fortune teller/We're as happy as we
can be/Now I get my fortune told for free."

There Must Be Some Way Out of Here: a collaboration, focus consciousness on saving the world, lifting ourselves by our bootstraps out of
    present labyrinths & onto the open levels... essays and drawings,
stories whatever by anyone who wants to take part & has the energy,
grace and certitude to go right to the point. "let us not speak falsely
now..."

Das Energi is my Taurus (Marx, Freud) masterpiece, a true collaboration,
tour de force of economic theory, written (and read) by the collective
unconscious. Property is out. Money ain't worth much to me. How do
things really work in the world today? We all know more than we care to
believe about the way energy flows... Which is all we need to know to
be healthy & happy. Send for your free copy today.

     and then there's Indefinite Pronoun...

We have no choice
ITS ANARCY OR CHOAS--
    We really do know what to do=
              Begin this second
Now - it feels so good
     fuck that girl
              you love

     What the hell--
We only have one life
 we might as well try to pass go--they can
keep the $200 dollars--we
 have a get out of jail card called
    --EVOLUTION--

          And now
          after all these years
          acid clarity
               without acid

Glory to God I'm crazy again

Everything seems so clear
    unless you are blind, deaf
  and more stupid then dumb
  you really do khow the
gasoline engine is killing
  us--
        The absence of breathable air
            is painful enough
       but to deprive the race out of the
     pleasure of the bike and Rapido Burro
      is counter-revolutionary, deseased
     and not enough fun---
"Its all so good living on the farm"
           food gathering
                building
              working in harmony with your environment

              (Alan)

    I seem to be many people.

"It's not really that you are many people--it's that we
    are all one."

It's not just up to me to decide   what points of view we take.
     And it's December 29--Paul Johnson by to invite us to New Year's
  Eve in Albion. Cat Mother (rock group) is moving to Mendocino and
swallowing Paul as a member. Good music will be at this party. And
many people--more than 100? Paul was at Altamont. I feel like I've
been there now, many times. And I guess I learned something from the
experience.
              Don't follow leaders, watch yr parking meters.
       Dylan's First Law, the corollary to which is --are you
          listening, Stones?--   don't lead followers

    This is getting jumpy
        Creedence following Let It Bleed following Volunteers
    map of Vancouver Island and environs on the opposite wall
      Carl (Capricorn) Carol (Virgo) me
                          rolling on the river

          rolling, rolling, rolling on the river

Keep on choogling.

                I wonder whose mind is reading me?

Here's some stuff that happened last night:
     Lots of grass. Alan's been pursuing/runnning from Lark for
two days. "Why are you running from me?" "I'm scared for my life."
He's scared of Tami, his old lady, than who he has fucked no one
else for more than a year, I think. Tami is a gemini. She clings
to Alan very tightly, says she wants one man to put all her energy
into, often suggests that if Alan isn't that man she'll just have
to go out and find him. Searching for an ideal. In Lund, on our
northern expedition, Tami got very upset one evening after Alan
had been paying much attention to lovely Sue. Ian, our gemini
skipper, ventured that for himself he couldn't physically love more
than one person, or something like that. Conversation ensued, followed by Tami attacking Alan for talking about love when he obviously
(to her) did not love Raven, his daughter. Much anger, deferred from
open fighting by Alan & me retreating to the car, the faithful green
bus, where we spent the night. At one point Tami and Ian woke us,
Tami said something about the Raven, Alan repeated to her some thoughts
he'd had during recent conversation with me, that she was still
somewhat fucked over by a childhood in the jaws of the Catholic church,
and that she was acting out Plato's cave myth bit: people cling to
their own chains. Nothing was resolved. Anger another day or two,
then considerable improvement in Tami's mood while we were in Vancouver.

Rapping on the floor of that green van, Alan and I got a lot of things clear... and knowing that even one other person is really with you and understands is a great source of strength when you're involved in ideas and actions that make most of your friends uneasy. You wouldn't think in this day and age that it would be particularly controversial to take a stand against monogamous relationships... but ideals die hard, and the less you have confidence in your ability to deal with an immediate situation, the more righteously you denounce that situation in favor of a nonexistent, imprinted, safe ideal.

Which cuts both ways. A polygamous ideal has no more inherent value than a monogamous one, what we have to do is phase out all thought-processes that put a distance between us and our immediate reality. Which most thought-processes will do, because immediate reality is so demanding, it's scary, it forces the mind to face the fact that it is not in control of what's happening, it is only half in control and must be as receptive as it is willful, And what mind wants to admit that?

Anyway, one thought our conversation drew out of me that night was that I do believe there are people who find their mates, one other person of the opposite sex who supplies them with all the energy they need from people, or so much that sexual love ~~relationships~~ with others ~~doesn't~~ even interest them. I believe some people do ~~find~~ have fully satisf~~ying~~ monogamous relationships. Maybe.

However, I know I'm not one of them, and I'm just as happy being whoever I am and doing it the hard way, trying to patch together an environment that's supportive without being stifling, that's exciting but not so tense I can't relax and enjoy it. Environment in this case = human environment, the people I'm around most, especially those who particpate most fully in my mind, body and energy.

So I'm not looking for the girl who will be everything to me. From my own experience with myself & my relationships, I feel fairly certain that some of the things I want/need in a woman directly conflict with other of the things I need from her, and the only way for me to resolve this conflict is to accept each person I love for who she or he is, and not try to force her (impossibly) to fill my every need.

Tami seems to me to demand of Alan more than Alan or anyone can fulfill; the Raven does the same of Tami, which problem is solved by dividing the Raven's energy among us, it's easier to take care of Yarrow for three hours and then Raven for three hours than to have to put up with either of them for six hours; and part of the reason for that is that they get bored of you, the more variety of attention they get the easier they are to please.

Which brings me to the word "consistency," which I've so often heard babies need. Who says so? Where did that assumption come from? Maybe they only need consistency if they can't get something else they need even more. And they <u>can</u> get that something else...

We can get it together... Okay, so Alan had been approaching/
fleeing Lark for a day or two, now was approaching closer and for
slightly longer moments, and meanwhile Tami wasn't saying much to
anyone and getting dark around the eyes, like a storm approaching.
So somehow there everyone ended up in Lark's small room, trying
to discuss the matter: Yellow Kid on the floor, half-reading Man
& His Symbols or something, Tami at one end of Lark's wall-to-wall
high bed, face close to bursting, holding back valiantly, Alan
at the other end, a few feet distant, distant, Lark beside him,
naked under the sheets, unselfconscious 'cause it's her room but
uncertain as to what's happening. What's happening? No one knows.

I throw the yarrowstalks, Alan admires the slowness of the process
but wanders off and falls asleep, Tami & Lark get to talking, very
careful, slow but accurate, direct, Carolanne is there for a while,
leaves, eventually the stalks announce: Splitting Apart to Obstruction.
It does not further one to go anywhere.
                                        Alan goes to sleep. Tami and
Lark talk long, make friends I think, things become less clear but
much higher, we begin to open our hearts. Yellow Kid & I pretty much
on the periphery of this action, we think and do, it is the ladies
who have the most experience in feeling.
                                        Alan woken from his sleep
to talk to his mother, calling from Acapulco.
                                        I show Thistle the
first nine pages of Time Between.
                                        Kay makes tea, Carolanne to bed,
Tami to her house to rescue screaming Raven (Alan sleeps on) me in
to talk with, lie with Lark, after we chop up some wood for the fire.

She feels entangled, slightly, glad of the talk with Tami, not
eager to get too caught up in a struggle that is happening between
two forces, neither of them her; meanwhile we touch and love but
still hold back, Lark now uncertain of timing as I had been for
days, tired and that's okay, I think I know (or feel) how Carolanne
feels but Lark uncertain and things are so nice these days I'm
in no way impatient; Carolanne reading over my shoulder doesn't understand about timing--I say it's the way things mesh or don't,
all the different forces moving from and to different places that
make a given moment right for a given action, or not...like an I
Ching hexagram... She says, but you're so premeditated about it.
No, I say. And think about how easy my words are to misunderstand...
Carolanne says she thinks of timing as something spontaneous and
of course that's right, that's the word I would choose too I think
but "timing" as a word in this paragraph seems to her coldly-thought-
out... People often get the impression from me that I think a lot
about everything I do before I do it, which is not at all true... I
give that impression because I often think out loud about stuff afterwards, sometimes I figure out and explain why I did something, but
the action you see was intuitive it's the afterthought that's rational,
I enjoy explaining magic, confident that awareness can only heighten
true magic's value, but I never think out my magic as I do it's
easier (it's necessary) to pull it out of the air. Timing is a sense.
My mind is mercury (merc in gemini, mars in virgo) and it writes, tells
the story, in Logos-concepts; but my life (sun in taurus, moon in libra)
is venus, my actions are born of Eros. Don't let my mind confuse you.

And back in my own (what's that?) bed Carol tells me she wasn't ex-
pecting me back tonight. She's very sensitive, and it's beautiful
and very helpful, we're more and more honest with each other all the
time & a certain amount of mind-reading is necessary to that (honesty
& the energy that comes from it one form of telepathy)--
                                                    our love-making
is also finer & more exciting & satisfying all the time
                                               and Carl has just
come in saying an exceptional dinner is in preparation, which is an
excellent sign that the state of the family is high
                         I like it here

My conscious mind clings
                    i'm having trouble going crazy

     want to go crazy because i know who i am and the next step
   is knowing <u>more</u> of myself... nothing to hold onto since everything
is either here or gone... so let go; something will open
             a blossom is a bud having a revelation

(music input: "Let it Bleed" on headphones, same song, over and over)

      maybe i'm missing dinner
   try it without my glasses
          arthur suggests i could regain my sight in 6 months
                                    or something better??
             the music is starting to get to me
      sexy purple visitor
      i'm not hungry

shit don't I have any subconscious at all? this is the most cerebral
             writing i've ever done
                         i need a lobotomy

          30 hours to 1970

          i couldn't drown if i wanted to

      i think i'll rob a bank

I grow more interested in flesh and less in newspapers.
Maybe because there's more flesh around. Alas the generations,
alas the creatures afraid to touch each other. Lucky us.

I have lived in Mendocino now fifteen months; the world is a
different place than a month after Don's death. Then I flew to
San Francisco, to attend the science fiction convention in Berkeley and find a place in the country to live. California seemed
the logical place to look, after New England or backstate New
York... and I'd ruled out the latter on the grounds that I'd be
too close to Boston and New York, too easily seduced by interesting
gigs, city gratifications. So I watched the second day of the
Democratic convention in the NY Avatar loft (the people there
fully convinced that Teddy Kennedy was about to become our next
president) and the third day on the floor at Larry McCombs' in
Menlo Park. Flying across the country from tv to tv, body soaring
while my mind remained fixed, I learned something of time-space
suspension. It's done with jets.

And then that delightful convention, with so much THC or horse
tranquilizers or whatever we were getting off on. Things became
quite ambiguous, real, intense, surreal and different. I ended up
deeply involved with Jerry and Miriam, and Bob drove me up to Mendocino for a day. It was foggy, gray, indefinite. It was clearly
my new home.

Miriam and I never quite recaptured the incredible high we got
off each other at first, I still love Jerry quite as much as ever
but find it difficult to spend time with him and Miriam, maybe because they live in Berkeley... not just in it, they embrace it,
and tho they're my kind of people I guess they aren't living my
kind of life. Funny how important that can be sometimes.

The "i"s are flying off the page here, and it's beginning to
bug me so much I may not be able to continue. There's a typewriter
repair shop in Fort Bragg that's excellent; tomorrow morning...

Funny: I guess I'm really affected by the appearance of the words
as I write them. If they come out all fucked up, I get a frustrated
feeling in my chest and stomach that's kind of like sand thrown into
my creative gears; eventually I crunch to a stop, in wretched frustration.

It's a new day, December 31, and I feel pretty good. News
items: 3000 miles and 15 months from the last time, Lark and I made
love again last night. Carolanne uneasy in sort of a double-reverse
reaction to the state of things (she'd been trying too hard--to the
point of self-doubt--not to be in my way. You can be in my way if you
want, Carolanne...); everything's more than fine now. A fight between
me and Alan--maybe our very first--I awoke this morning to the sound
of chainsawing nearby; and though I have used the machine a lot, I'd
never heard it sound that grating, that ugly. I think--really--that
we're very tuned into the trees here, and when a noise freaks them,
as certainly the chainsaw does (it's a machine-gun), their fear-revulsion
vibrations race through us. So I investigated, and found that Robin

and Alan were on their second day (Carolanne & I were in Willits
most of yesterday getting the dogs their distemper shots, so we
missed the chainsaw sound then) of cutting a clearing in the forest
near our house ~~in order~~ to provide Robin with green poles ~~with which~~
to build a shack for his concrete-boat ~~building project~~. I was ~~very~~
~~very~~ shocked--I knew they'd been cutting poles, but I really didn't
suspect they were cutting down live trees for their lumber! See,
around here there's more firewood and building wood than we could
all ever use, available practically free (you have to get a permit),
as a byproduct of the lumber company cutting in the state forests.
You get a slash permit, and you can go in wherever they've been cutting and cut up and carry away wood that's been cut and left behind.
It was on these very firewood expeditions that most of us became aware
of what a really wretched job the lumber companies do: they are truly
the rapists of the forest, not only for what they take but for how
they take and what they leave. You would not believe the careless,
vile destruction... it's illegal to camp overnight in our "state forests," but pillage and murder of our natural resources is the number
one industry in Mendocino County... in the Pacific Northwest for that
matter, maybe on the whole American face of the planet. What is happening up here is as bad as the My Lai massacre and black leaders
murdered in their beds by the wife of the attorney general (oh Char-
lotte...).

So I walk out in the woods this morning and find my brothers
engaged in the same rape; and I flip.

Robin I don't know, and I figure
whatever he's doing is probably under Alan's guidance; Alan meanwhile
has gone into town to look at the ocean. I speak with Lark, Carol,
Thistle, nobody really understands why trees are being cut down, it
seems that Alan has chosen to do that rather than use his truck to go
into the state forest and get poles (because the truck despoils the
enviroment with its gasoline engine). So Robin offers to stop till I
talk with Alan; and meanwhile I'm livid. Lark embracing me remarks on
how my heart is pounding. I get on my bicycle, switch into second which
didn't use to work to see if it's any better now, and the whole gear
system jams. I can't fix it. And up comes Alan, happy, back from the
ocean on his bike.

I point a finger at him, then realize how silly I
am and ask him why is he cutting down trees. And he says they couldn't
find any on the ground that weren't rotten, need strong stuff for this
boatshed, and that area was starting to be a clearing anyway. "Starting
to be a clearing?!" I rant and rave, and then announce that I'm going
to destroy the chainsaw. Alan grabs me, stop me from doing anything
rash, I tell him that if he doesn't let me destroy the chainsaw I'll
take it and use it on his house & belongings (12 trees lie murdered
in the grove beyond) we struggle he says I cannot destroy the chainsaw
that's irrational calm down I say it's private property (his) and why
not destroy it, I get free and go into the woods, take the screwdriver
from the chainsaw tools and start dismantling, breaking wires whenever
I run across them. It is very satisfying to get the blade and the chain
off, they are harmless without the motor; Alan comes, goes, Alan and
Tami come and she says she worked hard for the money they bought the
saw with and we should not destroy it but give it away. I say I don't
want to give it to anyone because it's a dangerous tool, it encourages
bad judgment and unnecessarily increases its owner's karmic load. If
you'd had to cut down those trees with an axe and handsaw, I say, you'd
have thought it out more carefully. Anyway we can't give it away, it's
dead--I pull out pieces of wiring. Tami agrees it's dead. They go away
again. Alan says he doesn't think I'm doing right but he's not going
to hit me.

Alan also announced that he doesn't have time to build a house (in BC)
without a chainsaw while he's also getting the food for us and this'll
mean a lot more work and I'll have to help him with his house and I say
I'm already committed to that anyway; it's interesting that time is at
issue in so many of these things, efficiency, western concepts of progress
vs east/west synthesis ecological sense of what's right. Do we have time?
Well as Alan keeps saying, we have the rest of our lives free.
                                                           Trees cut
down meaninglessly do not.
                          Carl (visitor from BC, on whose land we may
some of us be living) comes by, says he also was shocked at first by
the cutting of live trees but it's hard to judge a situation... I agree,
point out that in all this theatre we could each as easily being playing
other roles, Alan as chainsaw destroyer instead of me etc, we're all
very close in terms of consciousness and different people take different
roles at different times to help us all through the same changes, I
don't feel very righteous or ego-involved in the whole thing, in many
ways it was Alan's energy that he's been manifesting of late that gave
me the strength to resolutely do something about what I felt was an unsatisfactory situation. We just keep going through changes...
                                                           Carl started
clearing the brush, restore the forest by cutting up and taking away
what's down, make use of whatever could be firewood, keep the energy
circulating, care of the land, very good trip. I start cutting out a
stump (they cut them three feet up, very sloppy, wasteful, and there were
trees nearby that actually were too close together that they had not cut,
because they weren't aware of thinning especially and, I believe, the
chainsaw didn't give them time to think) with a swedesaw, sort of an
experiment, close to the ground and I haven't used a saw this way before
but it cuts fairly well, blade's dull unfortunately, incredible amount
of work and after a long time I have sawed through but missed, you see
what I mean, as I went around to get at the cut from a different angle
(because the blade would stick when it was in pretty deep) my cut curved
and so the point where I finished was not the point where I started, I
had to get an axe and chop through half the stump to finish the job,
which was the easier way anyway. But it's all yoga, patience, discipline,
education, learning about the swede saw, about the axe, about removing
a stump... I burned off some of my rough-edged energy, and that's good.
I'm not at all angry at Alan--hope he's not too bugged at me--we all
have to just keep working on each other and on the consciousness as a
whole or we'll never get anywhere. So far things are working out okay.
It's no doubt possible to push each other too far, but I don't think we're
there yet.

    Another piece of news: Playboy just called, and Jim Goode regretfully
informed me that the piece he'd accepted six weeks ago was now rejected,
the managing editor was tired of reading about Woodstock and, I suspect,
was uneasy about my essay's enthusiasm, got to toe the middle line you
know. Oh well, Jim's go ing to send me $600 as a kill fee, and suggested
I try the Atlantic, which I will, though I don't expect anything'll
happen. Once a piece that people like starts getting rejected, as often
happens with my pieces, I find they seldom end up anywhere... except of
course in my books, or in my own magazines... I'm constantly reminded
that I got started as a writer by starting a magazine so I could publish
myself, and that seems to be the way to do it. Carolanne was disappointed,
not about the money (we were s'posed to get $2000) but because she'd been
looking forward to seeing my piece in Playboy, it would have blown a lot
of minds. I really don't feel disappointed at all, though; I kind of feel
that the essay's rejection is an indication that the kind of thing I'm
writing <u>cannot</u> appear in Playboy or that kind of extinct showplace, even

when the editors want it to appear it doesn't happen, kind of like writing for tv, which you don't catch me doing. So I don't spend much effort writing for magazines either, or feeling disappointed when they
fuck me up. That was last year. Onward and upward. We have to deal with
the reality we find. I really am very happy.

And Outlaw Blues has
been sold to a mass market paperback house, so we'll probably have the
bread to buy the boat this spring anyway.

We already got egg in our
beer; what do we want? The moon? Fuck it.

Maybe last month I would
have enjoyed a Playboy appearance more than a good day in the woods
but-- joy of joys-- I really am changing; it's not just a matter of
who I'd like to be any more, but who I am.

What a victory!

Lark and I finally fucking each other again, and that
makes me think of all the times we haven"t:

December '63, when I went to L.A. as much because she said
she needed me to as any other reason I can remember, I really like
to be able to respond to cries for help of people I really care
about, makes me feel I have some reason to exist, my friendship is
not shallow. And I wanted to travel, wanted to see Lark. And Van Dyke
and Durrie, Toni, David, my family in the southland. Lark on the
verge of leaving town, she and Steve and some other Rounders living
in an incredible nothing shack in Hollywood, dirtiest suburbs I've ever
seen not grimy like a city but trashy stuff thrown around inside and
out, post-war cardboard housing, very strange. Lark came up to visit
me at Van Dyke & Durrie's, self-parody of a Hollywood house, high in
Laurel Canyon or above it, Mulholland, magnificent view, magnificent
good times I had in that house, good dope, loving people, top of the
world to you this morning Winston the airedale liked it too but this
particular December Van Dyke & Durrie were moving out, landlord, Lark
decided Van Dyke (Capricorn, one of my dearest friends) was the Perfect
Man, I still don't know how she arrived at that, seemed strange to me,
nice to see her and we necked as it were by the pool in the backyard
plateau that magnificent view and in Lark's car on Sunset near where
the recording studios mostly are but she didn't want to make love this
time, some reason, I don't know but it was okay, it's usually okay too
I can be impatient, we wandered around, Steve trying to score bugged
me because of the dead time involved, gave Lark a coat for traveling
to NY, I didn't need it, and looking for a good book to read I suggested
The Girl The Gold Watch & Everything she was dubious but I think she
did read it and liked it. Talked not much about Trina who had just
broken up with me for the umpteenth and final time or about being married
which Lark now was after having lived with Steve I think four at any
rate many years; talked some about being pregnant which excited and
worried her and who was the father? and all the changes young pregnant
ladies seemingly must go through. A nice time; most times are. Also
on that visit I think I went to Subud with Toni & much nice love, good
times with Paul Robbins and girl whose name I've forgotten and fantastic rap session up at David Crosby's, which I just discovered I've a
tape of. It's always nice to see David, Van Dyke, LA friends, now
scattered over the world as friends tend to be, wonder when I'll see
them each again?

March '69, in New York, poor Lark the Rounders to LA in the summer
and New York in the winter, that's no fun, staying at Ron & Joan's
very nice people I'd like to see again sometime but as will happen
Lark & Steve having no other home or money overstayed their welcome
and there may have been hard feelings by the time they finally left,
Joan a Tarus lady they often eventually feel imposed on and then
are quite bugged for a long time afterwards. But I liked it there.
Lark and I met to go to the movies of all things and when she got there
there was no room left inside the theatre and nothing else we wanted
to see I guess, anyway we ended up just walking down the cold street
and taking the 14th St bus from the west to the east if I remember right,
Lark very pregnant, and altho we were very much going to make love at one
moment we later didn't energy flow keeps changing and we can be so easily
just slightly but completely out of synch. She Sagittarius opposes my
Gemini tendencies loves me as a Taurus.

March '69, again, after me up to Bennington to see wonderful Rew pisces
girl met on plane out to NY that time, only met because we couldn't land
and had to go to Washington then take off again without having left the
plane and make it to NY during that dead space meaningless in terms of
earth space/time time pretty girl and I struck up a conversation fell
madly in love and I happened to have the keys to an apartment not far
from the East Side Airlines Terminal (where the bus takes you). Love
just keeps happening, ~~~~~~~~~~~~~~~~~~~~~~~~ Anyway saw Lark after return
from Bennington when Virginia Sims (Don's mother) and I dropped by
Trina's loft where she Lark was staying (Steve asleep) while Trina and
Kim visited the west coast (which I sort of felt they were doing just
because I was in the east, but that's all behind us now). Not much interaction that encounter; me in a hurry to leave NY and Virginia and Lark
talking about typing Don's book ms, this and that, if anything happened
I'm blocking it. Also I remember I ran into Steve that month in NY,
when Rew had just gone back to Bennington after a weekend visit and David
Henderson, John Wilton and I were listening to Allen Ginsberg free at NYU
he was absolutely superb the only poet I've heard read who sounds as
good as good rock but any way with our short attention spans we had
split in the middle for a private intermission and we ran into Steve in
the hot dog place at Macdougal and Third, good rap about something I
forget what now but it was a very high meeting and then back to Ginsberg,
I love David we have great times together. bopping. Can't remember if
John was with us: yes, he was, he is more memorable from later in the
evening when we visited Essra on the west side and she played us some
songs. That was also the confluence trip to NY when Essra, my next door
neighbor all winter in Mendocino, and I got together and made love in
my old apartment which Tim was living in, an incredibly fine moment I
still remember it fondly and that was the only time we fucked either
before or since, though the future still lies ahead... haven't seen her
since Woodstock. A Taurus. Too strong, talented, beautiful, sexy, sensitive to get any of those things together... yet. But watch out.

Alan just came in, happy, said he'd been going through changes for
hours, great rages directed at me, now he feels what I did was very high,
he's going to continue with his project but with the tools available,
we embraced a lot and things are fine, better than that, high.

      And now Tom has arrived, returned from the city, Creedence playing
and energy is peaking, it's great to see him, looks good, Judy still
  in the city but things are appa rently clearer and so on we go, wow!

Qualification: Alan is still furious at me, though he now accepts
and supports my action. He was planning to cut the cord to my electric typer (actually Lark's; mine quit) but that apparently hasn't
happened so far. Off to dinner at Chace's soon; Tom & I and Carol
jus t walked in are listening to <u>Let It Bleed</u>, we just saw a super
free school pirate movie, out on the ocean on Nat's boat, the
pirates snuck on board and then when they were discovered lots of
swordfighting and some people into the water. They were all ship-
wrecked after three years and stumbled around on the beach. The
film that came back today (more soon) ended with Valerie fallen over
a hill and her foot which is still showing attracts a passing stranger,
but it turns out to be a squash. So it goes.
                              "I got nasty habits..."
The Stones on this album have their energy together like never before,
or at least since <u>Between the Buttons</u>. It ain't so much what you do,
it's the quality of your energy. But there's getting to be things
you <u>can't</u> do... Stones free concert was not a possibility at its moment--
so you pay attention to <u>what</u> you do for practical reasons, and raise
the energy for art.
                 "Don't you think there's a place for you?" fantastic
 dancing Lark and Tom now I'm getting involved makes it hard to write...
    everyone's dancing
            new energy infusions all the time
           I pick up Aeko--these kids all like action, movement,
 stuff happening... like we like rock   high energy fun
       Aeko is becoming a typical Caladan spoiled brat--it's
 beautiful. He cries now till he get picked up... sometimes.
Before he came here he'd accept anything. Now he's learned
 from the other babies that if you want something you DEMAND
 it   when these kids get out on the streets, things are really
 going to start happening   I mean, who's gonna get in their way?
       Stokely said: "If you thought I was bad, wait till you
         see Rap..."

    WE ARE FORCES OF CHAOS AND ANARCHY

    WE ARE OBSCENE LAWLESS HIDEOUS DANGEROUS DIRTY VIOLENT
                          AND YOUNG

       EVERYTHING THEY SAY WE ARE WE ARE

              But wait till you see our kids...

    ⌐ You can't always get what you want...
            No, you can't always get what you want
         You can't always get what you want
           But if you try sometime
             You just might find
           You get what you need ⌐

                    The Rolling Stones 1969

(notes on a pad before leaving for the party)

   I'm beginning to get excited   about imminent 1970
     amazing, as it's quite arbitrary
     but after all--many people see the moment
     1970 as meaning something's happening
     --great change!--and therefore a sudden surge upward
   in consciousness is quite possible
       --and I'm feeling that energy
           imminent

(I Ching--coins--for the party and "1970":)

        The Cauldron   to
         Preponderance of the Great

          Supreme good fortune.
          The Ridgepole sags to the breaking point.
          It furthers one to have somewhere to go.
          Success.

10 minutes to 12 peaking on sunshine acid...

Okay gang, get this-- it's now

Year One

no more "1970" or any of that crap, arbitrary numbers
counting up from improperly-dated, inadequately-felt myth salvation,
it's now <u>year one</u> and it will always be year one (I got this
idea from a science fiction book, The Left Hand of Darkness,
pretty good), every Jan first we change not the present but the
dates of the past and the future.
For example, John Kennedy shot in minus seven
a year from now you'd call it -8
George Orwell fantasy thriller +14
(you can drop the +)
Stanley Kubrick 31

And meanwhile it's always year one, happy year one, all
that stuff that happened yesterday is a million miles behind us
we're here in the present
year one forever!

Extremists can also phase out months & day-numbers,
by referring to a date by its sun & moon signs
(I'll meet you at two o'clock on Aquarius/Taurus)
you could speak of the "second day of Aquar/Taur" if
you wanted, or better yet, 2:00 the next day would be
26 o'clock, Aquarius Taurus
the mind boggles

our sleep patterns will change

history books will sound funny

a sense of proportion regained

("Will you be running for re-election in plus two,
Mr. Wallace?"
"Fuck you, Mr. Cronkite.")

People will be able to forget about things that happened more
than ten fingers ago.
The future may eventually disappear altogether.
The present will always be with us.

Up against the wall, Pope Gregory and "calendar reform"!
Long live the eternal revolution!

It was a good party, a good acid trip--probably the best yet.
Days ago I offered half my kingdom and my daughter's hand in
marriage to the person who could get me high (things being
so incredibly high and clear already I was having trouble transcending them) and Rick Lane did it...
The party was in a fairly small house and lots of people;
Cat Mother played just the way a band should play in this new
world of ours: not so noticably "good" and clever that you sit
back and listen but instead
                    playing right along with the mood and
consciousness and energy of the place, the people present, reflecting
and amplifying and spreading around what everyone's feeling, a band
should be the instrument of collective emotional unconsciuus
            music part of the bloodstream
            it was always there and yet I scarcely remember
hearing it
            we all danced and danced so fine, Carolanne wonderfully
high and happy, Lark, Tom, Carl, me all up in that crowded attic which
one could barely leave there being only the one pair of stairs and
people jammed in front of it, I came and left sliding through the
shelves at the other end of the stairwell and lowering myself to the
steps
            anyway when the acid turned up there was really no earthly
reason not to take it, it being there and we so high already, so happy
   Carl and then me, Lark if Tom would and he would so they did,
Carolanne doesn't take the stuff because of her funny chemistry but
  because of her funny chemistry I don't think she needs it, she
  sure gets high fast when I take some
                              about contact highs, by the way,
I have absolutely no doubt that whatever lsd does to the brain/nervous
system it is a contractable state, I have gotten high when Alan's
taken acid and <u>before</u> he's gotten high! I think that we do have auras,
 nervous systems are electrical systems so an electromagnetic field
 generated by brain & nervous system seems a likely possibility, and
also that other brains would be affected by changes in nearby fields,
particularly if people are eating the same food, dealing with each other
a lot, intermingling energy fields and body chemistries. Such intuitive
"science" may seem true bullshit to serious-minded concrete thinkers
     but minds aren't made of concrete you know
            I arrogantly believe I may know more about bio-chemistry elec-
tricity physics economics (not as separate disciplines but as one)
  than most biologists physicists etcetera
                              mostly because I don't lie
to myself
            and I'm not afraid to think outside of what is provable
        or reasonable
                        anyway the contact high is partly a matter of
   smiling because someone smiles at you
                                but that's not the whole
   thing, the other night Carolanne was really tripping for hours
alone which means something chemical must have happened in her head
            and she sure didn't swallow nothing

            but back to the party....

(I'm playing Love's <u>Four Sail</u> album which I really like; I like it
so much I haven't listened to their new album yet, I'm still busy with
this one)

The acid came on slowly, very pure, we were dancing or sitting,
not talking much, it was kind of dark I guess 'cause you couldn't tell
who people were till you got close and sometimes not even then. I
couldn't tell if I was getting high or think about it much, I didn't
know how much I'd taken, just stuck a wet finger deep into the powder,
things were just sort of blending and flowing. I was a little concerned
about how many people there were and how it could be difficult to get
out (not so much thinking of a fire as just the conceivable need to Get
Out), claustrophobia but also having so much fun that I'd just look around
to see if the others were still there and tho sometimes one or another
wasn't, went downstairs for a while, there was always someone, and downstairs held no attraction for me, if I left it would only be from fear,
caution, and I didn't feel like admitting to myself that there was such
a thing as fear in the universe. All this time so high that no thought of
New Year's Eve what time is it? or any of that. Sometimes the music would
get so loud or frenetic that I would feel like I really had to leave,
but I'd hang on, like riding a bucking bronco, if you can keep your
cool and ride out the rough parts then things get relaxed again and it's
all really worthwhile cause the truth is you enjoy it when things get
rough if indeed it turns out you can handle it, it's exciting, satisfying, I like it when I can use my strength (and it's only fear, uncertainty,
that keeps me from that pleasure).

Eventually downstairs, after I saw Carol
going down a second time and it coincided with my feeling I'd more or
less had enough, uncertainty (claustrophobia) but also curiosity about
the rest of the party. Found Lark talking to someone from NY, standing
in a door from which came fresh air (oh yeah; it hadn't been downstairs
I wanted to go when I felt uneasy, but outside)--I investigated, but it
was just a bathroom. Incredible house seemed to have only one entrance
and exit. Lark was doing fine, so I rolled on. Found Alan asleep beside
the babies (Aeko and Raven), fast asleep on his back, feet sort of in
the air like he'd been sitting down and fell back, Steven Anapolski came
in and asked "Does he always sleep like that?" admiringly. I said something, but discovered I was too stoned to, like, complete my sentences.
Tami had been on the stairs as I came down them (many sitting on the stairs
and always people going up and down), looked fairly freaked but unapproach-
able, I just said hello.

I sat on the floor of the nursery (where Alan was
sleeping; there was also a couple holding each other lovingly in the
corner) and picked up a crayon, tried to draw what I felt and who knows?
may have done all right but I couldn't tell, eventually I found myself
putting down words on the picture, drawing them, so someone might know
how I felt, not confident of communicating just with lines, the words
said
so much energy   later Tami, outside, said she'd
seen & appreciated my message.

I went outside, said hello to this and
that, the house just bursting with energy, incredible, sort of stumbling
towards the back where there was a bonfire I ran into some people, a
couple, and we all three just embraced, held each other it seemed a long
time, maybe five minutes, very close, strong, nothing siad, then they
went on towards the door inside. Me to the fire. There was Thistle, who
hadn't come with us but later, I told her I'd finally got confused (what
I'd wanted all week) and she congratulated me. Seemed to be having a
good time.

(Are these pages of solid type hard to read? Do you lose interest? I'm just writing the stuff as it comes out, but I'd like everything to be accessible. Maybe it's just a matter of reading the long raps only at times when your attention span makes it comfortable. I know that there are books I like very much I can barely read, or don't finish, and I want to make it easy for my readers but not so easy that I don't say what I want to say. Dilemma. Well, for the moment I'll just carry on; we'll see what happens.)

Ron and K were leaving, did I want to go? (We'd come together.) Well, you know, I did want to go, get away from the energy, dangerous, scary, but more than that I wanted to stay, enjoy the energy, not miss anything, be with the people I really cared about (who don't include Ron & K). But I went to the car with them, to see if we'd left anything there, a baby bottle, coat, whatever. No. Okay, bye. I felt they left because the energy was getting too high rather than because they were bored, but that may have been projection. Anyway, **I doubt** I could have stayed myself, had it not been that I knew so many of the people there, which allowed me to see it was just us, the loud apocalypse music just some guy feeling just the way I feel and moving his fingers on the strings to express it.

Fear of the energy, so the question: what am I afraid of? becomes What _is_ the energy? And the answer is it's people, it's us, feeling good, feeling so good that we're an immensely potent force, which collective force in turn often scares us, as individuals.

In fact, within the family (this came out talking with Tami and Carolanne) one person is often scared of another person's energy, not that it's aimed at them, maliciously or otherwise, but that you feel you can't deal with it and therefore it's threatening to be around. As though someone you weren't sure of were always sitting there with a loaded shotgun.

The image of the party was that house standing in the flat west Albion moonlight, spiral of people going in, around, up and around to fill the two floors, reverse spiral flowing out, music & pure energy bursting out the seams so the whole structure was pulsing there in the night (yeah the joint was rocking, going round and round) bonfire in the back, further extension of the spiral as you went around and down going from floor one of the house to the fire. People standing around. Not saying much, only in the first floor living room and maybe kitchen were there many talkers, oh yeah also a few in front of the house, mostly people too stoned to talk though, not necessariyl stoned on acid but the energy was like sunshine explosion for everyone caught in it. Like Woodstock, exactly like the first Be-Ins or Woodstock, which in itself is amazing and satisfying, exciting news.

We're on our way/and we can't turn back.

Break on thru...

What else can I remember of the party? Well, I remember talking
with Eric & Alice, out front of the house, about Canada, drawing a
map with my hands, talking about flooded mountain ranges and fish,
Crown land and RCMPs and arable land. I was mighty stoned, but that
Canada routine is one I'm beginning to get down--after all we went
as scouts, certainly part of our gig is to report our findings to
the family. And they said they'd come by & visit... Albion and Mendocino don't get together all that often these days. We are none of us
automobile freaks. Ten miles means something.

                                        I remember Alan wideawake
and standing at the front door, Diogenes looking for the honest man
who borrowed (from Tami) his lantern. When we all left (Tom Carol Lark
Carl & me) Thistle was already gone, Alan was seeking the railroad
lantern (a much-treasured piece of Alan's Aquarian life: the flashlight
he took with him when he stopped working for the railroad, back in
minus four) and Tami, uncertain as anyone about leaving or staying,
standing by Alan... when a lot of confusion's happening, one keeps
track of one's family. Everyone seemed accounted for: Raven asleep
in the pulsing house, Aeko with Lark in the car...

                                                And so back home.
I had been talking with Carolanne, who felt very depressed, it was a
time of great highs and great lows, energy surging in, energy draining
out, she wanted to go home, exhausted and uneasy, probably straining
not to take a tranquilizer (she does every two days or so; she gets
hypertense and fears becoming hysterical; something happens to her
heart), frightened of the enrgy and catching herself in a trap: I
want to go home. I want to be with Paul. But Paul wants to be here.
I don't want to bring him down. I'm bringing him down just by feeling
bad. That makes me feel worse... Why am I like this?...
        Traps scare me, downward spirals, because they're the op-
posite of the magic powers of faith and optimism (seeing the best in
things) that are my strength, my pass card out of here & higher &
higher. Black magic self-doubt is a true threat to true-magic self-
confidence, doubt leads to destruction, faith to salvation, that sounds
funny I know but the words have been all screwed around so that they
seem to exist as abstract concepts, burn the concepts out of your head,
it's no good just to dislike the church if you still believe there is
a Church, the way to make an institution vanish is to actually cease
to see it.
        And I love Carolanne, and when she's in a whirlpool
then I am, we have to fight our way out and that's okay, the hard part
is she doesn't always realize that she helps me out of traps too, so
she feels guilty about "bringing me down" to help her out, it's a
tricky matter cause I sure don't want her to feel guilty but of course
it's true I don't want to have to help her too often because that's a
downward cycle too sometimes, the more help you get the less strength
you have (you get increasingly dependent) so the more help you need...
The problem is being solved, I think, Carolanne is really working on
her fear, her occasional doubts of adequacy... and her life is getting
better all the time,   less pressure and more pleasure and more satisfaction. She's going through changes, switching from
the college world of credit given for abstract accomplishment (she was
an art major) to the world here of credit given for making people high,
accomplishment that affects our daily lives.
                                        I love you Carolanne,
just call me when you need me, I think you're doing fine. (She's
baking delicious bread, folks; pushing upward every day!)

And so back home, Tom driving, stoned out of his mind but it's easy you know, you just stay aware and keep to your side of the yellow reflectors, let your instincts operate (might be pretty rough if you didn't know the territory). It was a nice drive, Lark's car, a true friend, it always gets her there.

And Lark, who was just in here, pointed out what it was about the party: you go somewhere and when things get beyond a certain point you can't go back, you can only go further, Woodstock was like that, you knew once you were in the middle of it that nothing would ever be the same. And--the acid helped, but it was the party energy we brought home--back at Caladan nothing was the same, the energy balance had shifted and every one of us was some-one new, more conscious, closer to each other, further/ More than any individual, the group had changed.

This report, inevitably, has many objectives; one I've really got to keep in mind more is that I want to clean house, we're moving to Canada you know and will be living a clearer life which means a lot less stuff. So there are a lot of things I want to clear out of my mind, everything in fact, the stuff I feel I have to tell someone I'll write down here, the rest of it I'll toss out, except of course the stuff I feel I have to hold on to. Up, down, certain assumptions of identity, pleasant memories... this and that.

I'll be taking a manual typewriter, a battery-pack cassette player and not too many cassettes, a tent, swede-saw, axe, adze, fro, hammer and chisel, hopefully just a small box of books, some personal papers (but not the four boxes I have now), a handful of clothes and what else? A few pots and pans would be nice, sleeping bags, I'll probably bring my mimeograph and some paper... God, that's a lot of stuff.

But it's a lot less stuff than I have now, so some changes are gonna happen.

Full report: I want to get this together more, so many flashes and experiences and I know if I fit them together a larger pattern will emerge; I have a very definite idea of what's going on, in my life and in the world in general, but I find I can't just rap it out, one two three, I have to build up a certain kind of momentum. I have to fill in some space between us before I can feel I'm making sense to you.

Basically, I see the entire economic political social cultural (psychological physiological) structure of the northern (N. America, Europe, the Soviet Union) world crumbling about us, I've thought about it a lot and I don't see how almost any of it can stand up more than another ten to thirty years. The U.S. of A. is close to total collapse already. Meanwhile, the entire planet (or at least the survival of human life hereon) is threatened by the imbalances man & especially industrialization has caused in the ecological order of life on earth. Human life becomes more frantic as the peril and dis-comfort of our situation become widely apparent. Some people change their life-styles in an effort to do right. Some try to change the eco-politcal structures in order to make change easier or possible. Many flip out in despair, cowering in closets or lashing out like cornered rats. And while/this is happening, an unimaginably major change in the consciousness of the species--not man, but all life on earth-- is taking place. We are learning how to act as One.

Lark & I didn't fuck each other again in early gemini, minus one,
mostly because we were together only on the phone. I was travelling
with Tim & Rosemary Leary, on the first leg of the great guberna-
torial campaign. We'd gone from Berkeley to San Luis Obispo, where
Tim gave a talk at Cal Poly Tech and I had an adventure with a
weird Scorpio chick; thence to Miami for a rock festival, sunshine
acid in the orange juice, the Grateful Dead and the Youngbloods as
fine as I've ever heard anyone; and then, because the cat who was
going to take us to the Bahamas wasn't around, on to NY. Where we
stayed almost three days, and Tim gave a press conference. It was a
hurried conference, because about an hour after it started we all
had to catch the only available flight (Memorial Day weekend) to
Montreal, where we were going to visit John and Yoko in bed. And as
the reporters started arriving and I did whatever my gig was (sometimes running the campaign, sometimes staying out of the way), I
finally reached Lark, who hadn't been in the night before. We talked
a few minutes--she'd had a boy, Aeko,   in mid-Taurus--and we
knew we really had to get together, but the press was asking questions
and things were a little tense (even Tim gets caught up in New York
energy) and there was the plane to catch... The conference went off
beautifully, the travel agency sent us to the wrong airport and I
spent the night in Brooklyn. I was exhausted; I didn't want to have
to chase around Manhattan after Lark, who was doing something that
night, I just wanted to lie in bed and that's what Dale and I did. The
next day we escaped across the border.

And finally early Virgo, Carolanne and I driving through NY on our
way back from Woodstock (where we'd met) to Mendocino, we pulled into
town early and went to see E.P.Dutton, Susan and Hal, and then later
Jac Holzman at Elektra, at which meeting I was offered more or less my
own record company and therefore the opportunity to learn that that
wasn't what I wanted (my "no" was as simple as the question: "Can I
do it from British Columbia?"), and finally I called Lark from the
midtown drugstore where Carol and I were reading what the magazines
had to say about Woodstock and she told us how to get there, very excited, and soon enough, East 90th or whatever it was, there we were.
And of course there was really very little opportunity for Lark & me
to make love, too many people we loved who just wouldn't understand,
Steve and Carol both jealous when Lark and I   went for a walk
around the block, out to a New York deli to buy orange juice, yoghurt,
cookies, embracing on apartment building steps, our lovers waiting
suspicious inwardly smoldering buried in the NY catacombs five floors
above us (back, left). Lark and I didn't make love and said goodbye
in the morning and Carolanne and I off on our epic journey and here
it now is Year One and we're together. Some of us.

Early in the morning, lying in bed, hand on my stiff cock, hand on
Carol's thigh, think ing about (inside) the dream I just woke from,
thinking about the words I'll soon get up and write, gray nebulous
transition world, time between, to be turned into reality if Carol
or I made a serious effort to start fucking each other, our beautiful
energy drama dance explosion, but this morning we just lie there,
dreams fading from my mind, I put on my glasses to look out the window , cock slowly going soft, Carolanne is so sweet and warm in bed,
gentle, I love her, tell her not to doubt I love her and she says
okay.

The moments roll on. Here's a letter Tom started writing me while
I was in Canada, mid-Sagittarius minus one:

paul, judy said to me yesterday i really miss paul, it will
be nice when he returns. and so i decided it would be nice
if i left some notes for you, play by play description of
what's going on.
first some excerpts from some letters i've written.

i feel like i have a very big family. i live most of the time
with ten other people. sometimes i live with other people,
like right now i mean, when i'm living with seven people...and
there are others of my family whom i rarely see at all. it's
really a fucking shame. but they have their own things to do,
they are all on adventures, and maybe we'll get together sometimes or others.

i've been staying in paul's house, he's in canada looking for
land. as i said there are seven other people, all big
people and i'm living here. it's really amazing to see
how another family works. of course it's different, but it's
the same things. we have a genetic family, i.e, eight people
who are blood close, and here there are none, just people like
judy and i, who are trying to put together a lost family, an
imagined family, the survivors of the breed, the liberated
people, attempting to realize thier liberation to its fullest
possible extent, every minute of every day. and it is so
slow, sometimes. we get stuck, we struggle, we die, we rise,
higher and higher. things are very up.

the whole thing at this house has been very easy, if some
what uneventful. paul tulley's son came up with some musician
friends and played one whole sunday at caladan. it was a very
high day. a lot of acid around...i danced for hours and hours,
just me and the band, it was so nice. the whole question
of living has become more clear in my head. there are two
things happening....one is survival, with style, the other
is fill your space, entertain yourself, enjoy your leisure.
in the land where there is nothing you should do, and no
guilt about not doing anything, there we can start relating to
each other so much more clearly, in so many incredible ways.
i feel sometimes here that people are stuck in a non-
relating world because they don't know what to do with another
person, their forms in relating are very limiting.
end of excerpts.

today is tuesday. i slept with judy for the first time in about
two weeks. it was really very amazing. many changes have been
breaking heavy on her head. too complicated for wordshere,
but it has been very hard for both of us, and we are not very
close, but last night i think we broke through a lot of things
and made love and felt peace for a while.

    (Paul: As I read this earlier today I realized I should have
    gone with Thistle on her one day trip to the city to help
    Sally bring back her baby--they're at Tung's, where Tom's
    Judy also is staying--to see touch talk with Judy. But
    Thistle had left. I didn't think soon enough. Maybe I'll
    go down later in the week.)

yesterday i resigned as head of the caspar community school.
it seemed the only way i could keep spending time here without
going mad. that letter [that Tom wrote about the school, and I
published--Paul] has really blown my mind, and i still haven't
figured it out. it's really a weird thing. i fell really
good about it, i'm glad people really like it, and a little
baffled by it. it's hardest to accept the good things about
yourself. i think it made me more aware of my position here.
if it's going to be a one man school, that one man is not going
to be me. the weight is too much, and i really don't want to
go on a martyr trip. i think any time someone is thought to
be responsible for something that i'm involved in, i become
mindless... the weight of responsibility lies in authority, and
authority robs me of my rights to do whatever the hell i please.
the question is, can we function, can we survive, can we be
happy, can we do anything. well, i think we can do anything
we want, if we really want to. which is also where it gets
very tricky and complicated, because who knows what they want
.....which is to say, who has peace. everyonce in a while, on
a particularly clear day when everything is happening together
and exploding exciting adventurous calm, i get a glimpse of that
peace, and at those moments i know that there is no roleplaying,
that there is no leader, that no one is doing anything they don't
want to, that we have taken the step beyond survival with style
and are now playing on the fields beyond, toying with the
evolution of the revolution. so i quit to join the ranks
of everyone else who is trying only to make themselves happy.
we are all teachers and students, we are all the directors of
the free school, that is the only way the school will survive
because i have made that choice. if i don't survive, i will die,
which is fine, even though each day i find more and more reasons
to live.

paul- just got your letter, my head is swimming, i rushed immediately
for the typewriter, i've never been so high in my whole life,
your letter just finished me, i'm scared stiff, my hands shake.
is it possible to be so high, to see the face of god and life to
be it. so much has happened, only parts will come through my words,
there are so many stories to tell. i don't even remember what i
said in the preceding page and a half, it doesn't matter, you con-
tacted me, we were together, it was written within a day or two of
your letter, a deep breath, a sigh, i can slow down a little. paul,
paul, paul......
lark arrived saturday night, straight from new york with all
her stuff, there was a flash, we spent the next day together.
judy and i had spent the night friday night together in your room,
and it was the first time we had been together really, for months.
sunday morning she called to ask me to take her out somewhere, i
told her i had told lark i would take her to the laundromat, she
got angry, it was a cruel moment, but there was nowhere to go but
forward, lark and i slept together last night, it was really fine,
she's a beautiful lady, she has a beautiful 7 mo. old baby, hooter,
who is very cooled out.

today is monday, she went to bolinas, be back tomorrow, who
knows what will happen there, but it's very exciting, judy is
incredibly high at this point, took acid early this morning,
i came to school, we had a long talk that was incredible, we
are very clear for the moment, whatever happens will be mind-
blowing. things are really starting to happen at caladan, it
was very dull before carol and thistle came back, or rather
it was just starting to open up, when they appeared. donald
is sleeping with, or was,??? phyllis, and playing games with
thistle. they (donald, phyllis and arthur) play a lot of games
i think, i find it very weird, but was unaware of it for a
long time because i was just looking for positive openings...
and after a while, i realized that not too much was happening.
i started thinking more about it. spent a very interesting
evening at the tulleys', a jug band rehearsal, i talked to a lot
of people individually, ross, jan eno, nancy tulley, but was
amazed to see them pretending to be a family, it's a good act,
very amusing, but not very warm. 3. raven is beautiful, but very
difficult to take care of. it takes all of the family here
to take care of her, it takes listening to a lot of crying when
she doesn't get exactly what she wants, she's so fucking alive
and active, you practically have to put on a song and dance
to please her, and it is worth doing, she's so solid. she's
had some very high days when she didn't cry once, and she's
sleeping a lot at night. the family at caladan is really going
to have to pull together to take care of that baby, it's a very
good force.

it was really weird going to caladan. so hard to feel i wasn't
abandoning the family here, but i'm sure in my heart that i
wasn't abandoning anyone, i had to get my head clear to see
which direction to go. i spent a couple of days wavering
back and forth, very unsure, insecure, knowing the only way
was up. i also realized that the leap into the unknown
was not so heavy, not such a crisis, not life or death, i had
been thinking about all those things, the leaps are becoming
steps, i feel the stride flowing out of my being, all i have
to do is follow it, smooth.

the school has been so high it's amazing. it really goes on
without me or didi, it's a very healthy baby, growing very fast.
the scott kids especially are such an inspiration. that letter
was the beginning of a fantastic adventure for me, it has taken
me away from here somewhat, but i have brought it all with me,
its life and breath are mine.

your comments about alan and tami were well received. judy says
she really understands tami much more, she feels they are alike
in many ways, and i think so too. she was talking today about
how she is living in the age of marriage, where one person is
supposed to satisfy all your needs, and we are pushing out,
as you said. she feels the expansion will allow less intimacy
between two people, but i don't feel that. it may appear so at
first, but that is because it is such a new idea, or rather not

a new idea at all, but a new reality, that here we are trying
to do it, actually trying to live that way, and there are no
rules and it's scary and hard as hell.

carol seems to be in fine shape as ever. it was really a comfort
being in your room.

i have been hoping more and more that there is room when you
return for me to stay at caladan for a while, i really want to
live with you and alan, it will make me very happy if it works
out that way. phyllis and arthur are leaving, hmmm, an empty room.

judy and i decided, or realized that we have to have another
house for the family, that it is just impossible for the school
to expand any more without more space. the duality between a
home and a community school is just too much. since this
morning we've found four possibilities. there is much hope.

seems like it's time for another installment, i don't feel
very excited or exciting. i feel a little sick. lark is sick,
so is her baby and so is barden. judy is in the city, she and
rich took the girls down to the plane (they're off for l.a. and
palm springs) (that was sat, today is tuesday)
rich came back yesterday, i guess he didn't like the city,
judy stayed. i have a feeling she may stay for a while.
i moved back to the school, more or less, on saturday, cause
i thought it was time to do that, but i've been spending
a lot of time there with lark. raven's back there now, everyone
pitching in to take care of her. it's really fine, i hope
tami has the sense to pick up on it when she gets back.
paul where the hell are you....you should be here, i hope
you are soon, perhaps you won't come until we stop waiting
for you. the rain has been steady for about two weeks, or
so it seems. it cleared up on saturday, the sun shone,
everyone went out, winter is really here.
fuck, maybe i can write more later tonight...........

                                        Dec. 3, 1969
                                        Lund, B.C.

Dear Tom:

     I've been thinking about you--and Judy, and the school,
but also just you--the last few days. We've been having a
very good time--we've been in Lund since Friday night, and
it feels very much like home. Lund is the end of the road--
highway 101--on the sunshine coast, mainland side of the
Georgia Straight, a small fishing village about 14 miles
north of Powell River (pop 17,500). There's a good harbour
here, and if we get a place anywhere north of here on the

fjords, that is, anywhere east of Malcolm Island, this would
probably be the harbour where we park our cars and load the
boats--if we still have cars at all. There are heads living
here. We've been staying with Anna (her husband, Joe, is tem-
porarily in The City... some city, any city) from Whitethorn;
there's also Ken and Sue, Ian (who's been our skipper--we're
going out in his boat again tomorrow to look at a place north
of here--probably we'll take some acid and spend a night or two
there before coming back to "civilization"), Fred and Doreen,
John and Pat. The heads...and they're not all dope-smokers,
actually--are not as freaky as many of our Mendocino folk--
freakier folk can be found down in Sechelt (and Gibson's Bay),
the peninsula south of here, a place very much like Mendocino
and very pleasant...we may spend some more time there before
back to Vancouver. The people in Lund are wonderfully adventurous
& independent. Sechelt already is experiencing the population
explosion, and it's a bit closer to The City; Lund, on the other
hand, would be a very nice place to live for a while while secur-
ing a site for the village. There's land for sale here, good
land, a little steep (44 acres for $20,000) but worth it and
it'll be worth more in a year or two, and/or places to rent...
And the place we want for our permament site may not turn up overnight. So one possibility is that Caladan might move up here in
April. There are many many possibilities. It's hard to put much
of the information we're gathering into words.

As I say, we're having a good time. Yesterday, Sunday, Ian
took Tami and Alan and Anna and Jim (from Sechelt, who introduced
us to people in Lund--he's a friend of Andy's from Montreal days)
and I in his boat to Turner's Bay, 7 1/2 miles north of Lund by
water, where John and Pat are caretaking an incredibly beautiful
piece of land owned by the chairman of the board of the Chrysler
Corporation! Pat's a fine cook, and we've been feasting, sitting
in front of the fire, telling stories and drinking beer for two
days. Alan went into the bay, the third time he's used his wet suit
on this trip, and got a ling cod, several trout and oysters. There
are oysters everywhere here, shrimp, salmon, herring, cod, trout,
perch...we won't starve. And deer, bear, grouse in the forests...
I climbed the bluff overlooking the bay, dreamed of building a
house up there, carrying up dirt to put in a garden atop the bluff
in the sun... the bay is beautiful, wide and clean and mind-
relaxing, islands in the near-distance, mountains with white caps
visible on a clear day, calm calm water but ocean, it has the beat
as Alan says, a little too tame for Tami but it probably won't be
wherever we end up, dozens of fruit trees... And John's getting
paid to live there! Only access is foot and boat. But power lines
are going in, our destiny is further north...

At any rate I'm really committed to Canada, to the southern
coast of B.C. We've learned enough to know it won't be easy to
find what we want, many are looking and many have already bought
and the land that isn't in private hands is hard as hell to get

ahold of... govt. bureaucracy is advanced, complex, up here.
But we also know that what we want is here, if we care enough
to find it and procure it, to commit whatever energy is necessary. The village is more real to me--and simpler, and more
attractive--every day.

It was beautiful on the water tonight...setting out in a
rowboat from John's in the still water, reaching Ian's boat
(anchored in the bay) and setting out, six of us, so close, so
happy, sky of stars above, phosphorous stars in the water beneath us, quiet constant motor, Jim on the bow, Ian sometimes
at the tiller, sometimes messing with the engine (the exhaust
hose was broken)...knowing it's December and Canada...I can't
get it in words, but I felt wonderful, and now I feel lousy because Tami is upstairs crying (Alan's at the pub) and my good
mood is blown and this letter is still barely begun; excuse me
while I swallow my anger and go and try to comfort her.

--pause--

Far out! I really did it--put aside my anger feeling and
tried to help, not just to the extent that I could then feel
"well I tried" but really tried, and therefore succeeded. We're
beginning to breakthrough... Ah! At last! I want to tell you all
about the interchange just now between Tami and me and then Tami
and me and Alan. But I'm not sure I have the energy. What it's
about is Tami is frustrated--sexually, and a lot of other ways
too, because frustration isn't just about one thing; anyway,
this goes back a long time and the basic thing is: Alan doesn't
satisfy her. But that isn't really it, the real thing is--she
isn't satisfied. She just puts it on Alan, naturally, because
Alan is who she expects the most of. But I pointed out that I
deserve the blame as much as Alan, since we're travelling (living)
together... And a large part of the trap she's in (has been in)
is thinking all her hopes have to be realized by Alan--within the
Alan/Tami couple. Which may not be possible...I don't know any
couple who fully satisfy each other in all the essential ways.
It's like saying: I've got to survive off what I can find in
this 4 ft. by 4 ft. area of this room, and starving to death even
tho there may be a refrigerator on one side of the room and an
apple tree on the other because you don't believe you have the
strength or ability to go beyond that arbitrary restriction.
Tami feels she's not good at relating to people... and that's
true, and I can understand being afraid of having to suddenly deal
with the millions and millions of people out there to get what
you need. But the whole idea of the family at Caladan, I realize
now, is to set the arbitrary limit of people you can expect what
you need from at at least seven, not one. The couple really doesn't
make it any more--if you just look around that becomes obvious,
one person to satisfy all your needs isn't enough (but we get confused because of the sex angle), we've all tried that and it
isn't working.

Etc etc. I'll report further developments as they occur, nothing's been solved yet but we're making headway. Tami is relaxing--taking time out--which is very difficult for her but we may be on the edge of a breakthru on that too, it's too soon to know.

Meanwhile I want to tell you something I just thought of, before I forget, which is that I think part of why I feel so close to you is that I really can accept who you are, what you're doing and who you're being, I really like it and know it and affirm it, and this in a way allows us to be extensions of each other, if I die you'll be looking out for my interests on the planet by being yourself (tho not of course doing what I would do--we're different individuals) and likewise I feel you're behind me on whatever I may do that I feel is right to do... Anyway I'm writing this letter to tell you that I love you.

Paul

Last night Lark and Tom and I made love. ("You may think living in the transition is hard, but ~~I sure like it.~~" -L.)
it sure has its points"

It's the fourth of January, Capricorn Sagittarius, mid-afternoon, year one. I've been lying in the bathtub, eating date bars and reading old fanzines. Fanzines are mimeographed (sometimes dittoed) publications put out by readers (fans) of science fiction, and by people who used to read science fiction and now read nothing but fanzines. Like all universes, fandom is more concerned with itself than with whatever caused (and keeps causing) it. I've been/reading fanzines because I have hundreds and hundreds of them, all neatly filed away in manila folders in the bathroom cupboard, alphabetical by editor...and the only way I can get rid of them, which I must do before moving to Canada, is to read them or at least glance thru them, just in case you know there might be something somewhere in one of them that I'll just have to keep with me for the rest of my life.
It's funny about possessions. Most of these magazines were printed in editions of 150 or less, and a lot of the ones I have would be worth a lot (a dollar or two, a quickened heartbeat) to whoever's around these days that collects fanzines (fandom's been with us almost 40 years; it has its own history, language, and of course, since most fans are bibliophiles to begin with, its many librarians, conscientious & enthusiastic keepers of the faith). So I can't just burn all this stuff, I have to find someone to give it to. Which means I have a responsibility. The energy preserved in these possessions must be passed on to someone who will appreciate & utilize it. But that's not really why I've been reading

this stuff in the bathtub. The truth is: I love fanzines. When
I was 14 and no one would talk to me I discovered this whole world
of people who read as much damn science fiction as me and who were
more than willing to talk with me about it, to interact with me and
accept me as an equal regardless of age.
                              That meant a hell of a lot.
And I really was interested in science fiction. But the capper was,
these people published magazines! For each other, for me. And anybody could play. All you needed was a pen or a typewriter; and if
you could add to that a mimeograph or access to one you were off and
running.
          No tests to pass.
                     And see, I was in the third grade when I
started my first newspaper (the Sunlight Herald; it saw four issues
over the course of two years). In fact, when I discovered fandom I
had already organized an SF club at Browne & Nichols (the day prep
school I attended in Cambridge) and we were already putting out a
publication.
                    That was Within, which also saw four issues over several
years, and like the Sunlight Herald had a fifth issue prepared but
never fully printed.

          So I have mimeo ink in my veins. I still put out a mimeo'd maga-
zine today (There Must Be Some Way Out of Here), and Crawdaddy started
that way; and in fact most of my ideas about magazine publishing,
and not a few of my notions about writing, can be traced back directly
to fandom.
              After all, chillun, there haven't _always_ been underground
newspapers. And as a matter of fact, I tossed out my closet-full of
underground papers without even glancing through most of them.
                                                        It's an
honor to do time in the bathtub on your way out.

          And I'm enjoying what I'm reading. Mostly it's idle raps by and
about old friends. One way fandom has ~~really~~ affected my life: it's
~~really~~ been a strong determinant of my circle of friends. Here at Caladan, for example, Andy Main (of Andy & Judy, who you haven't really
heard about because they've been down in the city trying to sell their
car) was very deeply into fandom for many years. Alan was never a
fan himself, but many of his friends have been, going back maybe 14
years to the days when he knew Trina and Chester and Bill Donaho in
New York, I met Alan/ and Tami thru Jerry and Miriam, who were going to buy Caladan with me back when it was for sale to us, and Jerry and Miriam
are ex-fans who I met at the sf worldcon in minus two in Oakland.
Donald & Thistle I know through Alan & Tami, so you can say that Judy
libra (a friend from high school) and Carolanne are the only people
living here who I would know if I'd never been a fan. Course you can't
say that either, cause it's totally meaningless, as sentences with
if in them tend to be; still, I wouldn't be surprised if half of my
close friends are people I know through science fiction or fandom, ~~through other friends who are fans.~~
                                   It's one of those granfaloons that
really gets into your life.

So we came back from the party, and we sure were stoned. We gave God five stars for his excellent flic.("Fellini makes boring movies, Godard makes boring movies, Antonioni makes boring movies...") I started chopping wood. Carl made a fire in the living room. Carolanne was bum-kicked about something. And she was cold and wanted a fire. And I didn't care for her attitude, or feel like keep trying to make her feel better by talking with her... I'd spent the last hour or so at that, and she was still coming on with the attitude that my fun was at her expense. So I told her there was wood chopped up outside if she wanted to make a fire. And I put on the Rolling Stones. "Gimme Shelter." Really sounded good. Fire being made, things seemed okay. I was at that stage of a trip where you keep thinking of something else, and then get distracted from that. So I dunno what I was doing, but I went outside for a moment to see if the record was so loud it might disturb sleepers in the other houses (one ayem). Didn't sound too bad, I went to the main house to check and maybe get some food and look in on Lark and Tom. Lark and Tom in bed in Lark's room (off the living room in the main house), Aeko asleep in his basket. Tom: "Why don't you join us?" Well yeah, that might be nice, I sat on the side of the bed, we held hands or something, but in my room we also have a bed, and in addition there's a fire and the Rolling Stones. The Rolling Stones did it, and after not much thought about how nice the Stones would sound and a little doubt from Lark about Carolanne, me just saying that we should do whatever we wanted to do, when you're stoned try to keep things direct and simple you know, that is if you're trying to make something happen, like a walk into the next room or a sandwich or something complicated (for an acid trip) like that, after not a lot of consideration Lark and Tom were on their way across the courtyard to Carol's and my house and as I came in just a bit behind them, having been distracted again or something, I saw Carolanne split in anger. I realized what it was, though I really hadn't been thinking about it--since she keeps saying 'I'm such a bringdown for you' and whips herself with it and I (this doesn't happen all the time, but once every few weeks or so, often during acid trips, because she feels left out) had decided the simplest thing would be just not to let her bring me down in any way and then she couldn't accuse herself of that--what it was was, she had wanted to leave the party because of so much energy, it made her very high for a while but then scared her and disappointed her in herself because scared and anyway she wanted to go but we didn't go until Lark & Tom wanted to go (well it was Lark's car; but also I felt we were all in this thing together)...and we finally did leave, she got away and what happens? I brought the party with me, I brought it right into her house, loud rock music and Lark and Tom full of energy, Carl more discreet, me hopped up and something obviously about to happen and anyway No Peace so she just had to split but she was also very angry.

Well with Carolanne off somewhere I wasn't at all interested in Tom and Lark, it's not just how much you care about people but who's demanding the most energy from you at the moment, and Carol's needs & mine in terms of knowing she was okay were a lot stronger than anyone else's as far as I could feel. So without thinking but(Venus)following my heart I went looking for her, walked around Michael & Kathy's, our neighbors, Carolanne's special friends, but their lights seemed to be out, looked up in Donald's house, looked in the living room and Lark's room and then cautiously peeking into Thistle's, not wanting to wake anyone & feeling a strong need not to invade privacy since that was exactly what we'd / been running around doing... Thistle came

out and talked with me, softly because Wendy her guest had the flu
and was trying to sleep, Thistle told me of how strange a lot of the
party had seemed to her, she sees things in a different way from
most people she says and it can be very weird, she saw strange ego-
trips of people more or less forcing acid on strangers (popping it
in their mouths), people playing cruel games with each other...
It bothered her and also fascinates her I guess. I couldn't really
get into the conversation because I was worried about Carolanne,
that she was going to do herself in or go off and sleep in the woods
without a sleeping bag or something, groundless fears but fears, you
know... Thistle suggested looking in the bus, so I went up there (the
Greyhound bus K and Ron live in) but no lights... I walked around
outside a little, checked Andy & Judy's little house, then went and
sat in the living room. I couldn't do anything to find Carolanne,
and I couldn't possibly get interested in anything else until I did
find her, Lark and Tom I saw through the window of our house listening
to the record and making love and it just seemed irrelevant to my
problems, I'd stick my head in now and then and ask if anyone'd seen
Carolanne and when they hadn't I'd leave again. Carol kept wandering
around; or rather he'd go to one place, and then feel the need to
either leave there or go somewhere else or both... Lark screamed
"Bullshit!" in the other house and the music went off and then on
again as Lark stomped in, I went to see if Carol had come back but
no, Lark and Tom were listening to "Midnight Rambler" and it seemed
to Lark that Mick Jagger or the phonograph or somebody had murdered
someone right there in front of her and it was more than she was going
to accept, especially since it was her playing the record, she said:
"I'm not going to be a slave to that thing any more!" She told me a
little later that she really envied me, because I had gotten to murder a machine (the chainsaw); she said she'd wanted to murder my
phonograph, maybe she should have, because it was murdering and she
was being seduced into listening/participating in this. I went into
a rap about the creative machine and the receptive machine, the only
reason to murder any machine is that man can't use it properly, can't
restrain himself from misusing it, what really has to change is our
consciousness has to rise to the point where we can have atom bombs
without misusing them, the tools are there, the energy is there and
the only way man can survive is to become aware of his own relationship with the energy or the universe, meanwhile however it might be
a good idea not to have atom bombs around, I dunno, I call the chainsaw a creative machine in the yin/yang I Ching sense of creative as
willful, doing something (receptive: letting something happen to you),
and I killed the creative machine rather than attempt to work solely
on consciousness because I just couldn't stand to see more trees die
in the time it might take to raise our consciousness to chainsaw-use
level. But the receptive machine... Well, the receptive machine is a
problem too, we're not really mature enough or aware enough for that
one either, the mass media, phonograph etc; that's why I had to move
the phonograph out of the living room into our room, it was being used
too indiscriminately, whenever someone wanted to hear something he'd put
it on with very little awareness of the others who would also have to
hear. As a result we were all jammed with an overload of music all the
time, even though no one person played records that much. Playing too
many records is as easy as eating too much snack food if it's around, or

smoking too much dope. Or buying too many books, long a problem
of mine. Writing too many words, I dunno... Anyway, the receptive
machine now lives in Carolanne's and my house, and we've both tried
to make it clear that all are invited to listen to records in our
house as long as they are discreet, use the headphones unless everyone wants to hear, put the records back etc. So far it's working
out okay, tho clearly Carol wasn't happy at having the party in her
house, and parties tend to go wherever the receptive machine is.
Anyway, if it's okay to murder the creative m (Alan isn't sure it
is okay), isn't okay to murder the receptive m? Oh yes, but I'm
not ready to do it. I am giving up reading Newsweek, though.

  I waited, tried to stay out of activity and raps and just focused
on her, and of course she came back, she'd just been in the woods,
I even walked past her at one point but she said nothing. When she
came into the house Lark and Tom returned to Lark's room. Carol
and I talked.

     (We're listening to singles: "Anyway Anyhow Anywhere" & "In the
     City" by the Who, "Ticket to Ride" sounding very good and "19th
     Nervous Breakdown" an explosion. Feel great.)

  Neither of us can remember now what we talked about, but we were
close, and eventually I pointed out that what Lark & Tom wanted,
and what I wanted, was for them (& Carl) to be in here with us. Oh
yeah, Carl kept coming in and out, very self-conscious about letting
us be alone and not intruding and stuff like that but also wanting
to be here and of course his bed's in the next room... I really wanted
him to be with us. At one point he asked, would it be easier for you
two to talk if I wasn't here? I didn't know. He left, and conversation
flowed more freely. Well, Carol and I know each other pretty well.
But I really think we should all--who live together--get to know each
other better, so maybe Carl should have stayed even tho it did slow
down our conversation a little. We're in no hurry. Carolanne (this
was after we'd been talking some time, and felt good with each other)
did want us all to get together eventually--but not tonight. I sort
of felt that it was just something waiting to happen. I also felt that
when I accepted Carol's viewpoint (I was kind of the middleman) that
made me feel Lark and Tom were kind of childish, and I didn't like
feeling that way. Not accurate, not true. But easy to feel. So with
Carol I argued their side. And then finally left, to go spend some
time with them (but no more friction between me & my sweet lady) and
one of the first things Tom said was Carol should take some acid for
this reason, and Lark said no, for this reason, and I said I didn't
really think she "should" take acid at all, and we talked about that.
You have to be able to keep seeing things from other people's points
of view, defuse anger or ego conflict with empathy, if you want to
ge together. I really wanted us all to be together, not in the same
bed this night if that was going to drive us apart, but together in
whatever way we were, could be, everyone feeling good & trusting &
close.
     Lark Tom & I talked and held each other; no move towards love-
making. It wasn't time. But we were high, energy flowing well, Tom seeing
us as the Trinity, making me blush. I announced my new gig: Professor
of the Economics of Energy, lecturing on the subject more or less constantly to whomever will listen to me. My travelling chair in Paul
Tulley's Institute of Motion.

Lark went to the bathroom and saw the devil. "Are you sure it wasn't Mick Jagger?" I asked. "It was, it was!" Rap about original sin...I don't believe in evil, you see, it's just part of that whole good/bad duality thing which has less place in my world all the time. The Stones at Altamont certainly made me feel they have no inherent evil or sense of evil but only an aesthetic awareness of how to play a myth to the hilt, beautiful strong alive aesthetic but not real, pathetic against a backdrop of not-in-the-script reality, not evil but just murder happening in front of them and between spoken words of confusion and impotent pleading for calm Jagger sang of murder and Evil incarnate and demonstrated for all that he's one hell of a guy but he doesn't know what's happening, art can sure get you high but it's no sub-stitute for awareness.

I gave Lark my magic necklace (made by Tom, abalone shell & papermate pen rings) to protect her in the bathroom.

Carolanne interjects "Like Tami!" when I read her the line "how to play a myth to the hilt"; I think she's right... She described Tami as really thinking she's a witch and putting on the role but of course she has no more control over what happens than anyone else, which is also the mindblower about Jagger, he can't really handle it! So go ahead with the myth, Tami, Mick, every-one, if it suits your energy, but we should all be aware enough not to be intimidated by good acting.

It is up to the audience to manifest reality. If the audience is frightened, fear is what's happening.

Dawn came & Aeko woke while the three of us lay there. I returned to Carolanne, who had been awake and tripping in her head for hours, and we made love like never before. I could feel Carolanne feeling my every touch throughout her body, her whole nervous system spreading out from one nipple. She came and came. I loved it.

Further!

Some further thoughts on the chainsaw incident: Carol went into the woods recently and discovered that the place where the trees were cut down is her magic spot where she used to go and sit on a stump and play guitar, she drew a drawing on a fungus there and Michael & Kathy found it on a mescaline trip and now it's not a lovely spot any more, the life is gone. And when I heard that it oc-curred to me that Alan hasn't spent much time in the woods around here, he's usually in the ocean and he wasn't here last winter, it's really the winters when one spends time with the forest. So that of course would affect his consciousness--you have to go somewhere and become part of it, share minds with the other life there, before you can have enough awareness to behave well, to do right by the life cycle of the place.

We must learn to do things more slowly, thoroughly, compassionately. We are so dull, so unaware; as we are now at last in the process of becoming conscious, we must be very humble, aware at least that we don't yet know what's going on, step lightly so as not to trample the life we don't yet realize is there.

Another thing: Alan is really torn by the fact that the concrete boat is to him a very high project, living trees were really needed (he feels), and therefore maybe he acted rightly... But what he forgets, what we all forget because we are so deeply programmed otherwise, is that the end does not justify the means. It really doesn't. In fact, there are no ends: there is only now.

So we must do right now, completely right, no compromises, if it's wrong to cut down trees then only survival is an excuse for cutting down a tree.

Of course, it's not wrong to cut down trees--if you know what you're doing, if you know how to thin a forest so it grows better even as you get wood from it, if you're conscious of the natural balance in an area and how to fit your actions into it, if you're really dealing with your needs and not just gratifying your ego or casual lusts... it is very bad to be "efficient" of human energy without preserving nature's energy at the same time.

The human race is hurrying to its own funeral. A drag-race. Man vs. nature = self-destruction. We all know this. Is there anything more important than that we should begin to act on this information?

The first step-- take a few years at this, if you like--is to relax and look around you. Become aware of what is beautiful, what is healthy, what is alive. Phase out bad trips--not the stuff that's real that we don't like, but the bad trips we inflict on ourselves. That includes governments, cities, economic systems, automobiles, divisive egotism...

World's finest advice: relax and pay attention.

(Footnote to Alan: You're me. And I love you.)

The five together now
    who met and came close
    as year one opened

            lsd
            grass in a love pipe
            found at Woodstock

        midnight rambler
        you got the silver
        monkey man
                you can't always get what you want

music machine
    word machine
   flesh ears & fingers

            but if you try sometime...
                what do you need?

food
shelter
water & air
attention
affection

            you justmight find...

What do you do?
I absorb and transmit
                    energy.

            four now
        not quite bursting
                but happy

            three suddenly

                    how does this thing work?

pull out the plug...

I don't know what it means. But things have barely begun to get crazy.

Holding firm, holding together, holding back, nourishing.

Judy may come up from the city tomorrow.

"three suddenly" was Lark leaving. She's mad at me. Or was. She was I think bugged at me already when she & Tom returned from the movies ("Whatever Happened to Aunt Alice"?). So it's probably not something I've done, but something I am. For the last month or two I've really felt that I am being myself, however people react they're reacting to who I really am so it's okay, it's real. If something about me (I think it's my ego (confidence, arrogance)) bugs Lark, she's right to express herself.

It's hard for me to respond to her anger; maybe I'm not supposed to.

Am I just doing what I'm s'posed to do?

Etc. Well, Carolanne went after Lark, and then there were two, and Tom and I spoke of this and that, and when we came to the subject of Lark, I found myself ducking under my bed

where I keep my "stuff," including files of correspondence. Lark Weber. Try to give Tom an idea of all the people she is, know her more fully, more understanding. I gave him the first letter I hit. Put aside the folder as Lark, then Carol returned. Tom still reading. This and that happens. I go to the main house for a Dylan record after Lark says the album I was about to play is one she particularly dislikes. When I return, people are talking about letters, folders, and the like. Lark thinks it's weird I save letters. I say something about how I've been keeping correspondence files since minus eight, and some rap about how for years the only thing I could write was letters. But those were the only people I wanted to communicate with, so it worked out nice. Fussing at the phonograph. Music: "I Want You."

I can't remember what happened then (block?) but soon Lark left, followed by Tom, also by me: I asked, "Would you let me know when you're not bugged at me anymore?" she said, "I'm not bugged at you any more." or something, my ear for dialogue is not good. Back in the door, just me and Carol, I say that with both the writing and the loving going so smoothly, I must be really overblown (egotistic) difficult to bear. Carol:"Why do you think I spent three hours today at Michael & Kathy's, and the rest of the time in the kitchen?" Good-humored, also true. I'm glad she knows how to regulate her intake. Too much is enough, my brother Eric once said.

And then I found out Lark had burned my file of her letters (and my carboned replies).

Changes. Well, why not? I was certainly asking for it; and the letters were as much hers as mine. I'll miss them, but then I'm trying to liquidate possessions anyway--especially the treasures, because the treasures are hardest to get rid of.

Grin and bear it.

I am incredibly arrogant, especially when I'm writing and I like
what I'm writing; and if other people like it too, then the sky's
the limit. And I need that energy, it keeps me writing once I've
started. And isn't that a good thing?
                              Who the fuck knows.

        The truth is, I'm really concerned about the idea of this
stuff being typed and printed on paper. Is it worth the trees?
        Are there ends and means involved here?

        I certainly don't want to create a market for more trees. But
I want my books to be read. This one here satisfies me and excites me
a great deal. I really see clearly that my gig is to affirm reality,
let you know that the changes you're going through are also gone
through by me and our family and probably a lot of people. I don't
so much want to put people through changes as to give them strength
and awareness with which to go through the changes that happen to
them. I just want to open my life to you.
                                And it feels like it's
happening, at least a lot more than ever before.
                                        But--and this really
is the only question, all you critics out there--is this book
worth the paper it's printed on?   Ask a tree.

Carolanne and I had a talk about my Pollyanna attitude that Lark's
burning the letters and Playboy's rejecting the Woodstock essay and
other recent difficult trips for me were really all for the better
(not to mention inevitable). I think what she was saying is that
suppression is bad, restraint is fine. And I think I can say that
it is conscious restraint I'm engaging in, but I dunno, other people
have gone through this trip of seeing everything in its best light
   --Ian did it, and I think Carolanne --
    and they aren't still doing it, well, what the hell, it seems good
I'll keep trying it. I mean, on some level I can really see that
if I hadn't shown the letters to Tom after I thought of it, that
would have been keeping them to myself, private property, something
that can't be shared. And if I'd tried to keep Lark from knowing I
was showing Tom her letters, that would be ~~~~~~~~ dishonest, game-
playing, not openness among the family, so scratch that. And if
Lark felt it demeaning or disturbing to be a folder, and so acted
on her feeling (we vote with our lives) directly and finally, hooray
for her. It all seems right, and I have that many fewer treasures
to hold me back. I really can't get upset about this.
        And I do miss the letters; there were some beauties. But she
left me the handwritten ones.
                        I love Lark

        (All yr private property
            is target for yr enemy
                and yr enemy
                    is we ...thank you, Jefferson Airplane)

Onward and upward... I fell asleep inside Carolanne. And in the morning (first day year one) or afternoon or whenever we finally woke, we still were high. Clear and soaring. Carl and Carol and Yarrow and Aeko and I went for a walk, to the river. Incredible sunshine day, seems like it's been a week of sunshine now, even as I write this it's so beautiful I feel crazy to be indoors at all, guilty (?!) at wasting so fine a morning at the typewriter when I could be just sitting under the trees.

From here to the river is straight downhill, maybe half a mile or a little more. There's a wide horse path that's nice to walk on; but this day we chose to wander pathless through the forest, impossible to lose your way--you just keep going down--and it was fantastic... it blew Carl's mind, it blew all our minds, no doubt good imprinting for the babies too, second growth redwood forest sloping downridge towards Big River, leaf earth branch brush mulch underfoot when you stumble it's like tumbling on pillows, absorb any shock so the baby doesn't feel it(I like carrying 'em; a backpack separates you ▬▬), the way the light falls through the trees is unbelievable, the way you suddenly find yourself in the middle of another universe & an infinitely beautiful and open one, like Alan under the ocean it's like taking acid, away from the path you really are inside the forest and oh so high, down the slopes the trees rise behind you and before you, burned out stumps of first growth here and there, Carol found one we could live in, better than a tent, I've walked this way many times and each time is utterly new, a different route, a different trip, more to feel, more to know, I and the forest change every day and we meet anew again and again and again. It is always a happy meeting for me--the forest treats me well.

Carl and Carol and I all so happy, the babies too and it's especially good to be with them when you feel so good. Aeko and Yarrow just soaked it all in.

We walked by a stream, the hillside folds into a stream every few hundred yards or so so as you walk down you're bound to run into one and you can walk along that for a while, baby gorges trees fallen across them sometimes no stream at all because the water runs underground, then a trickle again, you walk first on one side then the other as the brush gets thick, then up the bank back to the hillside which continues to carry you down.

We came to an opening, sky and sun on the slope clearing where forty years ago the trees were taken a bit more thoroughly than anywhere else, bushes here now, a good place to hold a midnight sabbat under the full moon, forest bacchanal with homemade wine and song.

Soon you can see the river.

And of course we'd stop here and there and just sit, absorb the wonder and if they invented a drug that could do that to your head in Lower East Side bedrooms marijuana sales would fall off to almost nothing...

But instead they rip up the forests to keep the cities going, steamboat Earth, we've burned all the furniture and the cabins and some of the deck now we start throwing planks from the bow into the fire because we got to keep moving at all costs...

strap yourself to a tree with roots You ain't going nowhere.

We reach the river/writing the last page turned me on so much
I decided to go for a walk in the forest/invited Lark, had to call
Susan at Dutton first/good, high rap; news Raymond probably on his
way, cross country by car, adventures/poor Raymond has been discovered, says Susan, by Hollywood/first Jerry Rubin's autobiography
and now this! Poor Raymond/but he's become a brilliant writer; he's
really saying and expressing where he's at/real/Carolanne Ron & K
back from town/mail: interesting article in EVO about A. Goldman
calling Jagger a fascist in the NYT, which article I also saw,
quite by chance/funny associative schizo EVO essay right on: of
John Mitchell's fantasy & Mick Jagger's fantasy the former by far
the deadlier/New York Times the journal of abstract conceptual distant "objectivity"/Goldman frightened clever obtuse/can't anybody
out there tell what is _real_? No, not as long as we keep reading
Newsweek and watch the evening news...real temptations for me (but
no tv)./mail: more pictures from Dale, dogs (afghans), bears on a
picnic, bears on the stairs and a news flash so much more real
than NYT that we reprint it in its entirety (you have to imagine
a bold type New York Times head)

THE FAIRY PRINCESS
 CUTS THE TAIL OFF
VICKI SCHULTZ'S PONY

(ny, year one; special
to _Time Between_)
     The Fairy Princess's
best friend was named
Vicki Schultz. They were
best friends even though
the Fairy Princess' mo-
ther hated Vicki Schultz
because she read plays
by Tennessee Williams
and acted them out in
her living room.   The
real reason was that
Vicki Schultz wasn't a-
fraid of the Fairy Prin-
cess's mother.
     The Fairy Princess's
mother made her swear
she would not be friends
any more with Vicki
 Schultz, which she did,
but they continued best
friends nevertheless un-
til Vicki Schultz went
away to school in Texas
and came back with a po-
ny. After that Vicki
Schultz didn't talk to
anybody. All she did was
ride around on her pony
and ignore all of her
former friends and ac-
quaintances, even the
Fairy Princess.

                    So when Halloween
          came the Fairy Princess
          cut the tail off Vicki
          Schultz's pony, not the
          whole tail, just all of
          the hair, which was even
          better because the pony
          and Vicki Schultz riding
          around on it looked stu-
          pid without the hair on
          the tail, so Vicki
          Schultz had to stop rid-
          ing around on the pony.
          Francisca van der Linden
          helped cut the hair off
          the tail with the Fairy
          Princess.
                    The End.

We reach the river, and walk along the river road/west,
towards the ocean, to visit the campsite where the houseboat
was last winter.

I forgot to mention that Moksha was with us. The dogs weren't
around when we left, but the first time Carl and Carol and I
stopped to look around & breathe in, Moksha came running up,
she followed our scent to an unfamiliar place & there we were!
Huckleberry (her mother, in heat again, the bitch) has taught
her the woods well. Anyway, it blew our minds, there she was &
we'd kind of already forgotten any one or where else existed.

"...I'm glad you are a monkey woman, too..."

          Today after I talked with Susan there was the mail
 to read and then trying to comfort Carolanne who's been in the
slough of despond, she says she feels like she's manic-depressive,
just caught in these downward spirals... But she did agree to walk
with us in the woods, so after maybe an hour of preparation or patience or just goofing off on my part finally into the woods, me
with Yarrow, Lark with Raven (Aeko home asleep), Carolanne leading.
Again, no paths just places to wander. The forest a wonderland
with bowls and ridges, incredible music, new rhythms patterns mo-
tions everywhere. Luxurious. Carolanne always foraging ahead,
it felt/she was running away from us (motion disguised but visible).

Why isn't Carolanne happy? I don't know. Because Lark & Tom & I
are in love? ...Maybe, because we're doing something and she feels
left out. But she knows she doesn't have to be. There's more. She
says she feels inadequate. God, she's more than adequate for me.
She puts up with my word riffing & weird self-consciousness (& my
ego). She's always interesting to talk with. She understands what
I say. She's nice to live with--her time patterns, the way she deals
with her environment, the invisible always-present stuff. And lately
she's really started to satisfy me as a lover, which was the only
thing I was ever unsure of... and I see her as more beautiful every
day, we really are getting closer & love each other more, we both
can feel it, the relationship is high.   What's wrong?

Something's short-circuiting her energy.

(Volunteers very loud on headphones) Michael Lydon on the phone just now, his report on the Stones tour for Ramparts (NYT couldn't hack it. Hmmm.) almost done, very exciting, I'm eager to read it. And he's writing a lot of letters. Says he's really realized the typewriter is his musical instrument, I'll bet his writing is becoming **great, very** rich and real, like Raymond's, like mine. It's in the air. Wonder what Wayne Hansen's up to? We've been out of touch, at odds sort of, but if anyone's likely to start writing genius stuff, he is. And David Henderson. Wayne McGuire. Chester. Maybe Chip, if he would just really let go. God, who knows what everybody is into? The energy **here** and Raymond's letter makes me suspect something fine is happening.

> Clarity is a good gig.

Break on thru. Michael told me this:

> Brotherhood and selfhood are the same. Coming together equals being yourself.

He says he's discovered revolutionary optimism. Right on, Michael Lydon! Maybe we'll come visit you tonight. It would cheer Carol up. Which is why I thought of and called you.

> There's a way that Carol and I together feel about Michael, which is something else from the way each of us feels.
> All feelings are good.

We walked along the river road...and then downhill, down the bank to a delta campsite,not where the houseboat was but one river curve before it, anonymous home lived in by many, owned by no one. Only a fireplace spot as **evidence** of man, that and a lot of strong audible vibrations, a "lived-in" feeling.

> The river is very inviting.

As we climbed down the riverbank I mentioned how I would sometimes swim **here** in the summer, spontaneous, your swimming outfit is always with you, somewhere under your clothes. And... I felt very **high**. It was a <u>beautiful</u> day, the woods had given us a shot of pure energy so clear I cannot describe and I wanted to go in the water. I realized I was in the act of deciding to do it, this was happening, and it blew my mind. Took off my boots and socks and waded. Cold but bearable. This is year one; don't speak to me of calendars. It was a warm day. We're programmed to think there are no warm days in January, so we don't notice them when they're with us. But I was clear, acid clear, forest clear, clear year one. Moksha watching ("Go on Moksha," said Carolanne, "Paul's going swimming. Jump in with him!") I took off the shirt Trina made me, blue jeans Carolanne decorated for Canada good luck, glasses... standing in the river water, feet deep in mud, taking it easy,am I really going to dive in? It's all **very** natural and wonderfully nigh but I can scarcely believe it. Thought of Don (drowned after taking off his clothes of an evening and jumping into ten feet of familiar water, something he'd seen me do at the same lake on acid the summer before...): what is about the water that attracts? Wading deeper and deeper, not quite to my balls, suddenly I dive, it's as easy as just doing it, not too soon, never hesitating quite enough to doubt... Shit! it's cold. But beautiful. Dive down, swim surrounded by water towards shore, emerge, clamber

to land, moving, whooping like Alan when he's just into the water
wow! jumping up and down, dancing, outrunning the cold what a jolt
of not just energy...awakeness. Now a sense of strength. I really can
do what I want to do, I can do it, I'm doing it, incredible, I really
thought I couldn't... no! I really knew I could.

. In again, another dive, swim, scramble to land, dance--and then
a third time, going down for the third time, third time's the charm...
I can't tell you how much this all meant to me, some sort of self-
awareness incident, primal strength awareness. Self-confidence. (Carol
today: "Where does self-confidence come from?" Tom, thru Lark: "The answer
is within you."/You discover it. Throw yourself in the river. Learn how to
swim.)
        ("Eskimo Blue Day" on headphones should be made available to
everyone.)

        When I came out after the third time, I climbed a tree. I was free.

        We walked back the river road, and up the horse path. The babies
fell asleep.

                        Today was another day.

        Lark and I finally just stopped, sat down with the babies on a
soft mulch slope. Carol on ahead, down the ridge still moving, not
with us, just ahead. Finally Lark called to her: "Hey, Carolanne!
Bring the joints!" "What?" "Come! Here! Joints!" She found us, and
we sat and passed the grass. Carol desolate. Me, I don't know what
to say, I'm bored of what I've been saying to her, she must be too,
maybe Lark will try.
        She did. Lark tries good.
                        May not have made Carol
happy, but I think she reached through.
                        Keep breaking that glass;
that's what lovers are for.

Carolanne said she felt she wasn't at Calddan any more, not in spirit,
where was she? That's not the question. She knows she's loved but she
doesn't feel she's loved. Wow, said Lark, that's what I was saying to
Tom last night!
                Love don't mean nothing if you can't feel it.
                Maybe you can't feel it 'cause you're wearing too
        many clothes.

It's my insecurity, said Carol. Everybody's insecure, said Lark. (On
the trip Carolannne said something about "a basic insecurity" and I
announced that basic insecurities would be a unit in our new economic
system.
        Carol didn't think that was funny.)

        I really think we'd all do best to learn to live with no security;
but looking at myself, I see I've only succeeded in phasing out a
lot of material security because I have another kind...being a "rec-
ognized writer", having a gig and getting credit for it, has given me
an enormous amount of security and I'm not sure where I'd be without it.

Carolanne, Carolanne, I've got to help you, what am I going to do?

And see, I realize that when you're caught in a downward spiral,
you can struggle and struggle and at the best just stay in the same
place...and that doesn't get you out, so often what you have to do
is let go, stop struggling, let yourself get dragged down as far as
you can go and through the vanishing point, whatever's left is real
and it comes out the other side...
    But when I see Carol going down it scares me, I reach out to pull
her back up. Should I struggle to help her, or let her go? She'll be
back, she's strong and smart and will emerge from the change happier
and healthier I know. I have to let go my fear, it's easier to say
okay let it happen for yourself than for someone else you love...we
are more afraid of losing our loved ones than losing our own lives.
I must overcome my fears, whatever they are.
Stay clear.
        Lark said, as we sat on the slope and talked, that we are
all alone, each completely alone and we have to face these things
alone but that isn't all she said, I can't remember it's just that
I've felt that too and I learned a lot of that from Mel, a guy named
Mel Lyman in Boston who says he's God and he is and you are too but
the difference is, maybe you (and I) don't know it, don't act on it.
We should.
Melvin, by being himself,will force us all to be Gods.
    I love him.
    Listen to this, Carolanne, Lark, this pulled me through after
Don died, this is the highest message I know of, from a book Mel
wrote several years ago, please listen:

        Loneliness is the sole motivation, the force that
keeps man striving after the unattainable, the loneliness
of man separated from his soul, man crying out into the void
for God, man eternally seeking more of himself through every
activity, filling that devouring need on whatever level the
spirit is feeding, the arena of conflict, be it flesh,
thoughts, aspiring to ideals, man searches for love to satisfy his gaping hunger, an ever INCREASING hunger because
the spirit devours flesh, exhausting every last outpost of
hope and the conquest must always necessarily search for
higher ground. The only pain is separation and the only joy
is breakthrough and the battle only really begins when man
has finally, through exhaustion, worn out every tangible means,
devoured everything in sight and arrived right back where he
started with an empty belly and a world with no food, having
cried all of his tears and standing completely naked and a-
lone knowing full well that there is no comfort outside of
himself, that he must walk that lonesome valley BY himself
with no kind words, no friendly faces, no helping hands, only
then does one begin to fully realize the meaning of utter
loneliness, it's difficult, it's the most difficult stage a
man will ever have to face and it is inevitable that all will
someday have to face themselves and make that terrible de-

cision. Few have ever succeeded as yet and those few
we call world saviours, our enlightened leaders who
threw themselves unresistingly into the black void,
learned the meaning of faith, and in time found a light,
their own INNER light, and WITH that light

they forever tempt us to follow

"Telephone communication
    only a three-minute elation
  when I hear your voice
    Through love & trust
    it's gonna work out fine
  The only pain I feel is all this
        time between
      you and me..."

Carolanne
Do not fear.
I am with you.
I cannot help you.
There is nothing to fear.

But it's very cold today...

here i sit paul and Carolann have gone to Elk
to see mikeal lydon and TD is mad at me because I.m
slightly drunk on korbell brandy

no longer manic diving in a 40 degree ocean has a
tendency to cool you out ,... even with a wet suit

listening to the greatful dead by earphones
too loud going to switch

Kay arrives and suggests I write Tami_Diane a letter

OK   Aletter to TD

I love you are my bright st star
the woman of my my dreams
m y psychadelic pioneer woman
my fish lover

please love me fore ver
as i forever love you

together with the help of our friends
we can bring both the dance and rythum of life
to level of hedonic exstcy beyond our very dreams

untold amounts of healthy orgasims fresh fish oys ers
forever   new wave housing our life a magical art
form THE REVOLUTION

we are the new nation the aqararian age
are duty and dedacation of
a high life full of meaning full work delight in
mind and body
our goal exstacy
without mental cobwebs or gasoline engines
we are overcoming the black forses of anger
and possesiveness

higher and higher
forever yours your master friend lover
and playmate

alan graham

Cast of Characters

Paul
Carolanne
Lark
Aeko
Alan
Tami-Diane
Thistle
Raymond
Donald
Tom
Andy
Judy
Judy
Raven
Yarrow
Ron
Kay
Michael
Francis
Barden
Valerie
Richmond
Carl
Michael
Katny
Matthew
Cynthia
Mitchell
Stanley
Gia
Bob
Bob
Spain
Mark
Sally
Rachel
Paul
Nancy
PJ
Jeroo
Gaver
Shuna
Robin
Judy
Bill
(more follow)
Tom
Pat
Shauna
Aileen
David
Adie
Ross
Jan
Dale
Susan
Hal
Jim
Ian
Jim

Location: Earth
(additional footage shot in
  Mendocino California,
  Albion Calif, Elk Calif
  ...addenda follow)

Additional Characters ("animals")

Strider
Moksha
Duncan
Smoke/Mouse
Huckleberry
Oliver
Legend
Shawn Rabbit
Hash
Kasha
girl
Miz Brown

More People

dede
Phyllis
Arthur
Robert
Becky
Stevie
Eric
Ellyn
Eric
Alice
Paul
Rick
Nick
Michael
Kathy
Joe
Anna
Ken
Sue
Bruce
Kathy
Sandy
Linn
Harold
Dolores
Laura
Beth
anon
Trina
Steve
Bill
Kim
Bobbie
David
Graham
Steven
Cheryl
John
Pat
John
Marvin

(camera slowly pans in on
                typewriter
         the sun behind it setting
          into the phonograph)

sound: Jefferson Airplane
       Rolling Stones
       Creedence
       Love
       Bob Dylan
       babies
       dogs

Executive Producer: God
   directed by I Ching
   costumes & sets by chance
      an Entwhistle Book

Trees are very important.

This I guess is very hard for manypeople to understand, especially
people brought up in a conceptual environment
where Very Important stuff is covered by the daily papers in such a way
that you pretty much know anything not mentioned
is not very important
   And it's hard, like if I wrote a book about how good trees are
people would say
               "Who wants to read a book about trees?"
      and   "I know how good trees are."
      and   "Right on! Far out!"

         and anyway, it would be a little like writing a book about
                    how good people are
                    printed on rectangles of human skin.

This is a book about how good people are.
I don't know what to print it on.

Trees are important for breathing. If one hundred trees
were planted
for every car sold & put in use on the earth
the internal combustion engine might be supportable
though it would still be silly.
But in fact
trees are cut down for highways
for prefab homes scheduled to fall apart on a given date
        to facilitate urban renewal
trees are cut down for avarice
trees are cut down for newspapers with automobile ads.

                    Buy me !

Would you believe a tree,
     even if I said it's not something I want you to purchase?

Trees breathe.
And what they breathe out, animals breathe in.
We're animals.
Automobiles exhaust a substance not useful to plants or animals.
Animals breathe.
Have you ever seen an animal breathe on a highway?

It just came over Huntley-Brinkley! Governor Blop has announced
plans for HIGHWAY EARTH   an Army Corps of Engineers Environment
Rehabilitation Project   (ACE ERP)
          in order to avoid dangers of skin cancer
                      and suffocation
            the government is going to cycle our atmosphere
                                 through a filter...
Impure air will be a thing of the past. In order to control a project
of this magnitude, it may be necessary
to pave the planet
                  too much oxygen   gets you high
     the Department of Health Education Welfare and Air
        will enforce strict standards
            there will be tree reservations
            for all you "nature lovers."
                  Trees after all are important.

I think I'd like to spread out and enjoy myself on this number.
At first I felt   very uptight, felt I should write nothing not
inflict my trip on you, all of you, but in actuality, I've wanted
to talk to you all for a long time(Paul just stuck his head in,
and I gave him a look calculated to drive him away and he left
much to my surprise. I shouldn't have cut him off like that.)
(Or was that all in my mind?) Hey Joe by Jimi Hendrix on the
record player, have to turn it off it bugs me so much. The
whole male superiority trip in that song makes me furious. I was (an)
married to a man who threatened to kill me if I ever did wrong.
To me it was like a dare.
     Carol Anne comes in. I feel I must ask her if she minds me
being here in her room. I know it's OK yet I ask. Still afraid
of Carol Anne. Don't feel as clear as her on a day-today what
the fuck do we say to each other basis. But I feel very clear
right now and it is because, Dear Reder, I have wanted to speak
to you for a long while.
     When I was in school I wanted to be a great actress. All
part of my theory that our consciousness as Life Artists takes in
many fields and tremendous telepathies between people. Like we
all used to wear work shirts and blue jeans and desert boots we
all looked the same, boy, girl, same now we're all different,
long hair the sexiest thing to happen in a hundred years. Itis
rxxix
     Now I have you in the palm of my hand what am I going to do
with you? I feel cheap and shallow standing here. Feel like I
better shut up but that is exactly what I decided not to do. Paul
has helped me a lot and it is obvious that his style of writing
has gotten to me,   because it's a way out--a way out of not
writing. Felt hung up all the years, where's the writing I used
to do. I just burned the letters Paul and I exchanged for the
duration of our love and it felt sooooo goood. Release from the
ego-trips of the past that bottle me up today.But I saved the
handwritten ones, to I don't know what they say. If I took the
time to sit down and push a pencil I must have had something to
say.
     Tom Brown I am thinking of you. I told Judy we are all
trying to free each other. Hard to speak about these people,
they will hear me. But there is no privacy(...ooh there ain't no
life nowhere...")
     The one who starts the dope smoking is the host. You propose
a joint and take the task upon yourself to actually roll it and
find a match. I have just offered Paul a pipeful of the grass
I found in his room in his pipe and he says thank you. Because
we are so stoned to begin with it is frequently something of an
effort to organize your ~~self~~ to producethat joint.
     I'm having trouble getting thru the coincidences between
whatcomes out of you and what comes out of the record player (If
you can just get your head together..")just showed Paul what
I had written because I felt frightened to go on. Please hang
on I need you.Naked throbbing lust. Blood dripping from her
teeth eyes enormous with Craving I want to devour you, because
Dear Reader is an ingratiating insult to address anyone, Dear
Reader indeed fuck that shit but it's me and you have to take
it or else you go away and we both lose
     So I have lieberated Paul's book(unintentional typing error
james JoyceLieber=love(German) no private property is the target

note from Paul: Carolanne & playing rummy / Midnight Rambler back to the game

Back to the typewriter. Tom and Francis talking today about
how the different instruments in the song motivating different
parts of his body, his body is making the music is his body is
a picture of the music. Until you are creating together--the
mass media, the mass mind. And The Midnight Rambler makes me
want to press my legs together and masturbate, if I really felt
free I would do it. Paul suggests if I need help he will oblige,
but it's not fucking , it's masturbating that is inspires and yes
friends I'm doing it as I write to you, I'm grossing you out
write here and now feel it "..and it hurts")
     I just think you should get more than one side of the
story . You see Paul and I don't always see eye to eye but
Paul is a fine fine man and I must speak no evil of him. hac2c
nowaeko is in my arms but i must keep on i must not stop for aeko
and thats why i dont deserve him i spend no time with him cant
stand the diapering and feedings and cries for lovethe only
solution is to include them as much as possible in whatever
youre doing . Not everything can go in the book you know.
Paul said of me, "She thinksthere's someone out there,"and i
said you have to act on the assumption that there is, and CAROL
ANNE looked at me.
     how can a book be someone's private property. thank you for
sharing so much with me paul. you. i find it hard to accept
your gifts sometimes. ill see you later friends. this is all in
the past by the time you read it my life no longer is like this,
but its been swell for me. sigh.

     sszss   a

     I thought that was the logical end but Paul has handed me back
     the piece of paper I am flattered how can I say no? This is a
     biography. I went to NYU where I went to a pot party my second
     week in NY and things were never the same. Or rather my college
     career did not unfold until as I had expected. It was all bullshit.
     Why should I talk about it. Rarely do I get good flashes of the
     past. I am disappointed in the past, bitter. All that love
     was so painful. I want it easier than that. And not guilty
     about it either. Fuck work. What is work. There's only living.
     The flow is gone. good by

<u>Currier, Carolanne</u>   born 3/25/-23 3:20 am Tacoma Pk, Maryland
        Virgo, Cancer rising, Sagittarius moon
        Bachelor of Arts Florida Presbyterian College -1
              major in art
father: Rodney Powers Currier, colonel USAF (ret)   65
mother: Mary Elizabeth Tolman Currier (employed by U.S. govt. as
              social security claims representative) 53
no siblings   female dog named Lucky   aunts
first lover: Albert Ganzenhubber, -4
favorite color: was green, now maybe gold
hair: brown   eyes: blue-green with yellow flecks, big
ht: 5'5 1/2"   wt: 112   contact lenses
job experience:
   waitress, Guy's Restaurant, Madeira Beach, Florida
   travelling photographer, John Hudson & Co, Greenville,
        South Carolina (now defunct)
   sales girl, Charles Bakery, St. Petersburg, Florida
   telephone solicitor (magazines), St. Pete, Fla
   assistant librarian, Madeira Beach Public Library, M.B, Fla
   check-out clerk, J.M.Fields, St. Pete, Fla
   temporary secretary, Cain & Cain (electronics), M.B, Fla
residence: Bethesda, Maryland -22 to -10
             Madeira Beach, Florida -10 to -1
             Cambridge, Mass. July, Aug -1
             Mendocino, Calif. Sept -1 to present

        You can't tell the players without a scorecard.

I thought I would also try to summarize the plot so far, to the
extent of my memory:

              Robin & Alan cut down some trees
              I took apart the chain-saw
              there was A Party & some acid was taken
              Lark & Tom & Paul made love
              automobiles were called into question
              Bob & Spain visited
              Alan was manic & then cooled off some
              Alan lost his railroad lantern
              walks in the forest were enjoyed by all
              much eating and fucking
              dope
              Alan interested in Lark
              year one
              Playboy rejection
              Tom & Paul write to each other
              Lark & Alan have their say
              Carolanne is unhappy
              Carolanne is happy
              Mick Jagger this and that
              the burning of the letters
              babies
              Tami
              Carl

Latest hot news:

                    Raymond is here!
                    Judy back from the city!
                    Also the return of Gia, Cynthia & Valerie
        (most of that happened yesterday. then today:
                    Andy & judy return (no sale of the car)
                    we go to a concert but arrive after it's over
                    walk by the ocean
                    dinner
                    a check to me for no longer reading The Economist
                    Raymond calls Susan in NY
            (and two or two and a half days ago
                    Carolanne & I visit Michael Lydon and read about
                        the Rolling Stones
                    Carol & Michael & I in bed together
                    Michael & Carol make love
                        (Carol's first love-making to Someone Else
                                    since meeting me!)
                    Carl now sleeping in Thistle's room but
                        one suspects they don't make love
                    Carolanne & I in bed together all Elk day after
                        Michael goes to the city
                    Carol came four different times in ten hrs, me
                        three times in less than that and
                                    the foam was at home
                    Alan fucks Lark
                    Lark fucks Alan
                    it is A Secret

        Judy Taurus turns us on to Ike & Tina live record
            good talk with her but better to come
                    Carolanne identifies with her
                    Judy sure looks sexy pregnant

            I like Raymond
            everybody likes Raymond
            Raymond is homesick

        Hash & Legend & Oliver all
                                    fuck Huck.

                    the babies are having a good time
                    the people are having a good time
                    the dogs are having a good time
                    the cats aren't talking

        Matthew makes good apple cobbler
                    Carolanne promises to make donuts
                    Carl promises popcorn

            abalone is better than steak

                        Ron is down, K hopes I can help
            I hope so too, don't have the nerve to try yet
                    hard to deal with glum people,
                            maybe they want to be glum
            but it's partly cause he's not smoking cigarettes
                    a hero of the revolution

late flashes (Thursday Jan 8??):
        Carl & Carol
        Lark & Paul some more
        Raymond's Michael arrives three ayem
                Raven sleeps through the night

<u>Rudin, Kay Adele</u>   born 12/23/-24 11:30 am Cleveland, Ohio
        Capricorn, Aquarius/Pisces rising, Pisces moon
        1 yr at Cleveland Inst of Art; semester at Mark Hopkins,
                Brattleboro, Vt; semester at Maryland Inst of Art
    father: Herman Alfred Rudin (died -16) (stock & bond analyst)
    mother: Alma Freda Hildinger Rudin Aegerter (55)
    no siblings   Greyhound Bus
    first lover: Rob Moody, -7
    favorite herb: ginseng
    hair: nondescript blonde (when the sun hits it it has rainbows in it)
    eyes: blue   ht: 5'6"   wt: 125   everything works
    job experience:
        wrote for freak newspaper West Life (Cleveland) -10
        rasberry picker, Cleveland, O.
        carhop, Manners Drive-In, Clevland
        sign painter
        secretary to a shoemaker
        record salesman
        free lance art crap (drawings at parties etc)
        modelling
        animal tending service
        freelance discography for musicologists
        weird letter clerk for railroad insurance company
        cartoonist, Hi-Brow Greeting Cards, Cleveland
                    (with *R.Crumb*)
        dope-dealer
        dope-farmer
        posters
        miscellaneous freak advertising, Baltimore
        sec'y, Clover Horn Chemical Co (witches' supplies)
        underground comic art ("Ishmael" in Yellow Dog)
        maintenance crew, Woodstock & Dallas pop festivals, -1
    residence: Bay Village, Ohio -24 to -10
                    Brecksville, Ohio -10 to -6
                    East Cleveland, Ohio -6 to -4
                    West Cleveland, Ohio -4
                    Brattleboro, Vermont -4 to -3
                    Baltimore, Maryland -3 to -2
                    Shrewsbury, Pennsylvania -2
                    Hartford, Connecticut -2 to -1
                    San Francisco, Calif, Berkeley, Calif, Pt. Richmond,
                        Calif, Oakland, Calif, Pleasant Hill, Oregon
                        cross-country via Prankster bus to White Lake,
                        NY, Dallas, Texas, San Francisco, Calif (the
                        Hunger Show), Mendocino, Calif
    (subject notes that after a certain point location & occupation
      become nebulous & irrelevant)
    living with Ronald Shea (q.v.) since -2

Andy and Judy back, I'm very tired but want to get some of this
down. Lark hasn't been here long, her room formerly Phyllis'
and originally Andy & Judy's, before Andy turned a chicken shed into
a fine little house, half bed and storage, the rest standing room,
desk, stove, good skylight and windows. So some of A&J's stuff in
Lark's room, stored under the loft bed, and they were in there today
retrieving some of it; I mentioned that Lark wanted the stuff out
of there, this turned out to be projection on my part, I'm really
into trimming away excess stuff (and 90% of our belongings are excess) from our living quarters, I don't so much mind outbuildings
filled with belongings because you could always forget them or
burn 'em down (or let 'em mildew) but stuff that intrudes into
our daily lives is particularly offensive to me, the channels of
energy hemmorhaging, leukocyte possessions clutter stepping over
boxes and people's feelings tied up in inanimate matter, the circula-
tion finally ruptures breaks down clots and so Let's get this stuff
out of here!
   I was nowhere near that heavy, at least I hope not,
tho maybe all that stuff was visible in me just under the surface
anyway, Andy reacted quite defensively, "We were here first" and
silly things like that but I hadn't meant to attack him just nudge
him because I know he wants to get the stuff given away and it just
might not be as high on the priority list as if he knew it was in
people's way, Lark has spent the last few days struggling with
clutter in her room, so I assumed but what the hell
         Andy came in and
made it okay and it's okay and also revealed that he felt I was
pulling rank on him, that had been his reaction, what went through
his mind was that I pay the rent and I was telling him how things
were around here and what to do. Alas, same defensiveness Donald
feels or felt, I am practically unconcious of rent-paying or money-
handling as part of my gig at this point, in fact I've paid the
rent for the rest of our lease period (April 30) now so that can't
hang over anyone's head but money just doesn't mean to me what it
means to Andy and Donald, I guess on some levels that's hard for
them to believe. I do feel like I can speak for a number of the
people here now, which is an ego-maybe-even-power trip I'd better
watch out for, I think I'm just trying to ease communication but
often I may be projecting and putting my own trip on people as tho
it were the family trip and get with it buster, that's bullshit I
realize and the temptation is always there, it's probably better
for me to keep trying to contribute to situations rather than defensively withdraw but I'm always nervous when I think I may be
going on an actual power trip, very self-destructive you know and
the thing that people are really afraid of when they say they're
afraid of ego-trips; ego-trips are just harmless masturbation or
honest self-appr eciation or whatever unless they are used to push
people around, subtly or otherwise. What I want to do within this
family is help express, make clear, the collective will or needs of
the family, but there will always be a distance between who I am and
who we all are as one, so keep an eye on me, don't let me pull any
bullshit.
   And please, no one get defensive any more about money,
the fact that I earn it out of proportion to the rest of us gives
me no rights whatsoever beyond the rights we each have, which rights
are extensive and should be exercised as necessary. When I speak my
mind it's not because I have some sort of status that allows me to
speak my mind but because anyone & everyone can & must speak his mind
if awareness & the health of the family are to continue to rise.

Andy also announced that he and Judy are not planning to go to
Canada with us. Carolanne had told me that Judy before they went
to the city this time had said to her that that seemed to be how
it was, but that seemed vague to me so I left it vague in my head,
now it's clear and open.

A little background: Judy is an old friend
of mine, she went to a girls' school in Cambridge that got together
with the boys' school (Browne & Nichols) I attended for plays and
stuff. We first met in -6, at the Solomon's house, famous hang-out
for some of us at that time, Judy was swimming in the pool and I
was carrying some Dave English manuscripts and doing something with
Jerry Friedman, possibly also involving a manuscript as I was working
on some magazine or other at that time.

Judy and I met. She was a
good friend of my first love (not lover) Franny & later (December -6)
there was sort of a triangle happening that culminated in a New
Year's Eve party where Judy met my best friend Bill (whom I had dragged
unwilling along). They were first lovers & lived for each other for
years and still are very close tho neither of them knows how to deal
with it, Bill's touring the world and Judy's here living with Andy
who she met here, they both came by last summer, at different times,
went away and came back to stay, & then found themselves staying together. Judy has been a close friend not -lover whom I see three,
four times a year for many years now, she and I tried being lovers
this summer and couldn't make it, now she's living here and I scarcely
know her. But the wheel will turn again...

Andy is also an old friend
but not someone I'd known that well, a science fiction fan, we may
have met in Chicago in -8 but mostly we always just sort of known
of each other and met, with mutual friends, in Camb ridge, NY and
(last year) the Bay Area. Andy also knew Alan, before this summer,
and is a close friend of Bob Lichtman's, who is very tight with this
family in so far as he can be, living in the City. I don't know how
far that is...

So Judy is one person now, with Andy, as has always
been her way: she completely involves herself in a man and is un-
reachable when with him and very clear and attractive and intelligent
when apart from him (though often depressed). Uh, she's one person
now, and was another one this summer, and another one when we in-
teracted before this summer...so I don't really know where she's at,
except that she's fully and sincerely on Andy's trip and Andy doesn't
want to go to Canada, i.e. a more survival kind of life, cut off
from city energy and a lot of the things he's into. Andy also said
he feels that he's going in a different direction from many of us
here and that the two trips can't be incorporated into one, he mentioned as an example his and Judy's food explorations, they eat no
meat nor fish and are trying to get what they eat straight for them
in a number of ways, this is difficult when you're living in a place
with a communal kitchen and no one else on the same trip. And little
space in your house... Very true
(Lark just came in to tell me I'm missing THE culinary
event of the year one, I think it's Carol's donuts so
goodbye for now)

dear judy- i don;t know if it makes any sense at all talking
to you about what i want to talk a bout,i get very confused
when i talk to you sometimes. i think i understand alot more
where you really are. not only that i feel i accept it much
more. the problem is in when i get sucked into your fears and
paranois, for a long time i didn't know what to do with
myself in alot of ways and you gave me alot of direction.
but you're a really different person than i am, and that's what
you've really done for me, show me who i am, gave me the confidence
to be myself, and in that way i've given you alot too,=
but i have/had other things to do besides you, and you didn't,
maybe i'm not the kind of person who settles down with one person,
or maybe i just have alot of adventuring to do.i guess i don't
think deciding that kind of stuff is important, i guess what i
think is important is what's happening now, and feeling good
now. that's selfish and i guess that's why people get hurt.
you really blew my mind on that acid. it was really a breakthrough,
i was really out of it the rest of the time down there, but
as soon as i got back, i did a bunch of work here and went out
to pauls, it was new years eve. it really clicked when i got
there. lark was there but she was mad at me because i went to
see you and was very cold to me, but paul was clear as ever,
and i felt together again. i'm really connected to the people
at caladan.thistle, lark, tami, alan paul, carol ann. lark
 has moved into phylis' old room and is getting settled, she is
very much a part of that family. alan wanted to go to bed with
her, tami freaked, there was a confrontation, paul threw the i ching,
with yarrow stalks, it took so long, alan fell asleep, tami
and lark started talking, caustiously, and it seems came to a good
understanding....that is..lark won't sleep with alan cause it
would cause too much hassle for everybody, tami is relieved, alan
is trapped and going through incredible changes. he was on a trip
about not using gasoline engines, but spent one morning cutting
down a bunch of trees near the house with the chain saw...paul
got very mad, they were green trees, all close together, carol's
favorite spot,and he took the chain saw aprt.
anyway it was christmas eve new years eve, caladan was invited
to bill chases for dinner and were going to a party at jan me's
old house, did i want to go along. no, not at first, but then
i realized that i did want to goalong. we got in a hassle about
vehicles, i said we could take the green bus, but it turned out
francis wanted it in case he wanted to go to the party, i realized
i'd had the bus for a week, so we scrambled around and it worked
out fine.   dinner was nothing, except walking to bill's house
in the dark, falling in ditches getting lost...tami seemed really
freaked. got ot the party alot of people we knew and alot more we
didn;t. rick lane had some acid, paul took some, lark said
i will if you will, it was all so perfect...she was the one who
set me up for the acid trip with you. for some reason she made
me want to get high, though i'd been thinking about it for a long
time, then i was with you, that was perfect too. we got very stoned.
very stoned. the music was upstairs in the attic room, it was jammed,
but still in the back there was plenty of room to dance if you wanted
to, and i did. there was an incredible amount of energy, paul
said it was like woodstock,i felt really good, very sexy,
i wanted to fuck so many people, but of course i didn't. it was
the same frustration

of every party, no climax, no ¢l¥ release sometimes i was really
scared, i had to kiss of alot of things, i felt i was letting go
of alot, that it was really someting just to stay there.
midnight was very nice, feeling so close to so many people,
that kept me together, there were alot of people i had very good
connections with. didn't see lark much, she was wandering too.
paul was very high. carol ann freaked out early, wanted to
leave, was mad about something, paul disappeared from view.
another thing, there was also alot of people into very heavy
black magic trips, very down, but they weren't in control,
it was obvious, and considering how many people were there,
probably 300, it wasn't too s urprosing...well a little after
midnight, lark came up to me and said i have to get out of here,
and though i could hardly talk, or see, or think, i knew she was
right, it was time to leave, but how, what did we have to do....
it seemed impossible....somehow we did it, found the baby,
¢b¢ told alan and tami we were leaving, alan was ranting around
because someone had taken his beloved railroad lantern, his
most prized possession, and tami was terrified, but sticking
with alan, as we were walking away who should appear but paul.
then to find the car, all of a sudden it was in front of us, we got
inside, her car was broken, we had to push it to get started,
and somehow we got back to ¢l¢ caladan. i was more stoned than
iwas on the spagetti.the rest of the night was very fine,
talking to paul, listening to music, the new stones, fucking,
alan came back very late, tami stayed all night, i'm still not
sure what happened, or what she did all night, but she
returned in the morning with raven in one piece. carol ann
freaked more, i felt really good, strong. i got up early
and went for a walk, still very stoned. the woods were really
beautiful, i could hear a few birds, and then in the distance
a chain saw,,, a very wierd twist, all night and all that day,
every time we got fire wood i would flash on the chain saw,
or rather the lack thereof...it affects us too, i was counting
on using that saw... it really makes you think about things,
the scotts did itwithout a chain saw, it's a matter of time
sense.do we have time to cut all the wood we need by hand....
if not what are we doing with that time, and is it worth
more than the machine. i really don't know what to think.
it makes alot more sense if i think abut living in british
colombia that it does in mendocino. it's seems the machines
are so abundant here, to stop using a chain saw would be ridiculous,
we still have cars, electricity, refrigerators. the whole day
was incredible. it was like we'd all been through a real storm
together, and everything was alright, everyone was still alive,
and things were continueing. lark and i made coffee cake,
karl, a visitor from b.c. made a porridge.   i called here and
talked to francis.   he and the kids had taken mescaline, he
talked about you, about my sticking it out with you, working
with one person, anyone else would be very incidental, rather
infrequent things. i felt he was insecure, that he doesn't want
to lose either of us. i went though alot of changes too, for
a while i couldn't understand why i wanted to be at caladan at
all, but then i realized that i was trying to hold onto somethigg
because it was a base, a home,but you can't keep things by
clinging to them, only by letting them go. i was doing what
was making me feel good and i realized i would go on doing that.

i have alot of energy and i want to do alot of things and
be deeply involved with alot of people. i'm not so afraid of
working things out now, used to be that whenever you were
feeling bad or i was feeling bad it was a major crisis and
I had to do something. well now i know things are going to
work out...i don't know how, when i think about you're coming back
i get scared sometimes still of course, but i know i can trust myself. i think francis is also not too hot about the b.c. idea.
he really wants to do that electronic thing in navarro. i think
it's a really good thing, i'm just not sure i want to stay around
here, there;s so many people. you know francis can handle that,
it doesn't even affect him, but ireally like the idea of the
wilderness, of building from scratch, but then the school
, i'm not sure where that's gonna fit into things.....
i came down here that evening. things have been really
really nice here. very quiet, barden seems to be in really good
shape, she and i have gotten much closer in the last couple
of weeks. i really like talking to her. i saw how she and
francis have worked things out. i mean i could see the duality
in what they said,/and did, i could see tham as too very closely
connected people...it was a very nice vision.
rich and madeline are having a beautiful affair, they both
look really good and happy, maggee was here tonight to tell mad
to be ready to leave tomorrow and she said she wanted to stay,
at least for another week, maybe for good, it means alot of
hassling with her father for maggee, but it's so good who can deny it
mathew is/was depressed about it. he really doesn't dig being
the younger brother and losing out all the time.
today was saturday and a really incredible day. barden and i
both decided it was the day to wash and wax the floor. so we did.
bonnie has been here, it's been really nice having her here,
she helped alot today. we moved alot of stuff around, waxed
the floor with two kinds of wax, and buffed it with an electric
buffer that sue had, she split up with gordon again and is
living in the back , the two girls spend most of their time over
here. francis also finsihed the dark room roof-floor, finished
moving the fort up there too, i built a platform extension
off the loft, over the kitchen for the kids to put their clothes
in. the floor looks fantastic, really beautiful.   there have been
alot of visitors through, but it's been very easy. i guess when
the pressure of the school is off, we're much more able to handle
other things. school starts again on mpnlday....i realized
tonight that what would be really great would be to have another
place to have the school so we could live here, because it's
really/agreat place to live...i wonder what it would be like
if monday came aroundand none of the kids showed up for school
wierd. i have the feeling i babbled alot but didn't really
say too much....i don't know, i can never tell if what i write
is good or interesting, i should write more...oh judy i wonder
what's happening to you...i hope you're happy and feeling good.
maybe i'll come down next weekend and take some more acid.with
you. i love you. fucker.

a few things i forgot, listend to mother earth all day, what
a great album, then as i was writing this letter we were
listening to the beach boys, 'friends and '20-20, they're
really fine. i wonder how your belly looks, how the baby is
how big your boobs are, if you got all your stuff, //
paul was by today, he helped on the floor, asked about you,
was mad at himself for not going to the city with thistle
and sally to see you. keep on truckin......

Well toms gone to larks, and here i am - alone? no, not really, since

its all supposed to be a state of mind, and ive got me, and needless

to say endless admirers. i sit down to write whats in my head and am

stumped as usual after the first line. its that first line that always

makes me sit down at this typewriter, and after the first line i
i become self-concious, and wonder if anyone will read my mind and
if so what should i say to make things interesting, and if not why
am i writing anything down. o.k. another first line, maybe an entire
page of first lines, one nighters, ill become a hollywood star. The
room looks good, i like the chaos, the look of movement in every
object trying to find a place or have a place found for it. Jim looked
at me today and said," so your a free woman now." "I said, " how did
you know" he laughed and said "I could tell by your eyes." He said
your baby is going to be a boy, but sharon did some little magic and
it predicted a girl. The magics been right twice out of two. well at
least it will have a sex. thought of going to see lark today, wanted
to be able to say goodbye to her, maybe even hug her, but my usual
fears persisted so i didn't do it. i guess the grapevine

cthis is tom speaking now, midnight rambler playing, lark dancing.
judy and paul, aeko and raven all in the same room, everyone very
much on their own trips, wi.hch is   fine with me, i really don't
feel like being into anything with anyone, it gives me time to
concentrate on myself. it appears tnat judy is going back to the
city soon. it's not working with us she says. i wonder. sometimes
i feei very responsible, sometimes i don't. i can oniy do so
much. part of it is that i don't want to let francis down,
ne really wants judy to stay, and it will mean tnat i can't make
it work. but what can't i make work? i naven't done anything
wrong. I get so frustrated trying to make her realize how much
she is loved. she really doesn't want to believe it, too much
too accept. the hardest part of yourself to accept is the good
part.

        What is all this bullshit. Its all so clinical. is it
possible that youve all become practitioners of the human
mind. What happens when your mind turns to jelly, oh happy day
tom in love. lark bridging the gape between paul and tom. lovers
from your first acid trip together. so happy im leaving for the
city, but we love you. stop taking about it, make me feel it,
im ready, where are you...right over there. strike the last
paragraph. its another emotional outburst.

        Look Judy (this without reading the above) there's
something I want to find out from you--
                you're the person who's most dissatisfied here
        I think and so you probably know
                                what has to happen
        do you see what I mean?
                        don't think that everything's fine and
        there are all these trips here and you just have to
                        get out of the way
                and we'll all keep going
        because whatever's happening isn't one thing & what's
                happening to you is a part of it too
                and has to be brought into it
        even if it means blowing apart all the apparent solidity
            of things because nothing's solid
                        if everything isn't being dealt with
                health means the health of the whole organism
                        this isn't intellectual I know you're important to me
                        I don't know who "me" is
                something has to happen

                okay now I read what you wrote
                        ?
                        what can I do?
                        maybe one of us knows, that's why I
                                have to talk to you

At which point we took some acid...

Early in the morning I start. The second day of the odyssey. Carol and I are on the road, contacting friends, spreading the gospel, working for Entwhistle Books. Tom off to work (Grove Valve & Regulator), Aileen asking questions. This is the essay part of the quiz. In the latter part of the "20th" century Robert Anson Heinlein wrote a book called <u>Stranger</u> <u>In</u> <u>A</u> <u>Strange</u> <u>Land</u>. Discuss.

Since that last acid trip I have not worn my glasses.

Identify: Charles Manson, Mel Lyman, <u>Harold</u> <u>and</u> <u>the</u> <u>Purple</u> <u>Crayon</u>, <u>Red</u> <u>Planet</u>, <u>The</u> <u>Martian</u> <u>Time-Slip</u>, Sirhan Sirhan.

What is the Rolling Stones' aesthetic? Be brief.

Who do you think you are?

*

I just took a shower with Aileen. Aileen is four. She and her sister Shauna take showers with all the guys who come to the house. I lie here trying to imagine a world in which that would shock anybody. No. There is no such place.

Tom's typewriter is throwing me for a loop. For the moment I'll just stick to pen. I don't have a lot of confidence in my ability to write by hand. Like Phil, who thinks he can't do it without amphetamines. I'll bet there are people who write only with the tv set going.

Is a bit of confusion prerequisite for creativity?

*

I'm not confused. I know what I'm doing. I'm keeping in touch with my far-flung friends, I'm gathering manuscripts that need to get published, I'm playing Mel Lyman's music and presenting his face and   words to everyone I know who might not be afraid of him. I'm writing a novel called <u>Time</u> <u>Between</u>. This is the essay part of the exam.

Consciousness is high. High Good Times (LNS)

Weatherman article. Good perspective. I have
a gut reaction against "Weathermen," violence as
an ego-trip is not my aesthetic, especially when
guilt-driven and media/fame-oriented. Weathermen
seem to me deranged intellectuals, neurotic
still, responding to a System which most of us
don't even see any more (no flesh on its bones)...
Richard Nixon and the Weathermen deserve each
other, they are acting out roles no one else
would these days even accept.But solidarity...
I embrace the Rolling Stones, naive and arrogant,
and I'll embrace the weathermen too tho it ruffles
my pride, we're all in this thing together and
let's get one thing straight: Goddamn it, you've
got to be kind.

     Right on, Eliot Rosewater! And here's a
code I've found for myself: don't murder. Not
yourself or anything. Killing to eat is not murder.
Killing for the ego, the emotions, the intellect...
is.

     Mick Jagger will now unsing "Midnight
Rambler."   "...swallow your pride; you will not
die; it's not poison." (easy for a Gemini to say)

     Murder is what Sirhan Sirhan, Charles Manson
(Weathermen too speak of them in the same breath.
Hmm. Well I affirm my aesthetic, no matter what
bedfellows it brings me.) cannot be forgiven.
Murder is what the weathermen and Rolling Stones
will have to stop prattling about. Don't they see
what they're doing to their karma? Yet the Stones
and W-men are honest, that is what we all must face
up to and realize; and Sirhan and Manson are strong
and courageous men--and courage is activity on
behalf of mankind--they must be respected. Embrace
what is right, cast out what is not as it should
be. Even tho both seem to come in the same package.
Remember: we are all Robert Heinlein, Richard
Nixon, Sirhan Sirhan. We must embrace what is us,
what is good, discard only our bad habits. To throw
out the baby with the bath would be to pretend that
you and I and Charlie Manson could somehow be
separated. We all have the same
                    unconscious
                         you know.....

When are you going to realize that the
Stones aren't gods? I could be talking to myself,
I suppose, but in fact I'm talking to my friend
Bob Lichtman (whose typewriter this is) who wrote
in a recent fanzine:

> I'm particularly down on the Stones for
> putting such a bum vibe on the Bay Area
> in particular (with Altamont, the Hell's
> Angels as cops) and the United States in
> general (their entire concert tour is
> marked by their appearing late at most
> all concerts, causing much uptightness).
> I find an uptight and evil vibe in much
> (though not all) of their stuff, so
> I've set them aside for now.

and

> Things had gotten to a pretty high
> place the last part of 1969 and then the
> Stones came along and bumkicked the
> entire region...

Bob, that's just ridiculous! When are you going
to realize that we're all gods? You really think
the Stones could bumkick an "entire region"?
That's giving them a lot of power
in _your_ head, at least. I just hope
(and assume) Jagger and most people learned from
Altamont precisely that the Stones do _not_ have
power, not the power to get what they want, certainly not the power
to control anything.

What's music? It exists only in the impact
it has on us, right? Does Stones music make you
want to murder people? Look to your soul.
& thank the Stones for letting you know.

I'm not saying listen to the music if you don't
want to, if it doesn't make you feel good, if it gets
in the way of something you're trying to do. When
you're giving up cigarettes, Marlboro commercials
may be a little much. The strength to shut off/shut
out what would make you weaker is part of your
godhood. This is all transition.

But blame the Stones for _revealing_ a weakness
in the Bay Area, in all of us, that we were trying
to gloss over and forget? To deal with and uplevel
reality we must face reality, the process of making
things higher does not involve hiding stuff in the
closet (where I found the Stones lp I'm now listening
to), it is a process of transcendence and it involves
discovering that we don't _need_ violence and violence-
talk...never mind what you don't want, cold turkey's

not an answer in itself, the only way to kick
heroin is to get more satisfaction from something else. If heroin's the best high available,
I affirm it.

        I don't think it is.

       So: do you agree we're all in this to-
gether? That means that the Stones & the Angels
& the people who went to Altamont & (ahem) the
people who didn't go to Altamont share equal
responsibility, i.e. awareness, for whatever
went down? Don't you agree we'll have to all
stick together if down is not where we want to go?
I know Steve is a beautiful person but watch
out for that touch of fascism
        it's there in all of us
  sure it makes sense not to play records full
of hate and killing (but if you'll look closely
I think you'll see that the Stones have never
hated), not to go to bummer movies
             but
   it doesn't make sense to pick and choose
who among us shall enter the kingdom of heaven,
    <u>that's</u> not where Christ was at
      and I don't think Steve means
to say that he'll only embrace the Rolling Stones
if they do what he thinks is right...
    naive & arrogant, the Stones and
       Steve Gaskin too...
     Mel Lyman
     Charles Manson
      Sirhan Sirhan
     Valentine Michael Smith
  me & you

  it's an interesting posture, honest
  tho annoying

"Dontcha think there's a place for us?"

    I do.

Let _It_ _Bleed_ is, to me, the peak of rock
and _roll_. Of course that's all behind us now
(almost, almost) but I still find it hard to
believe that one could resist listening to it.
It's like refusing to read Shakespeare (or
sticking to the Comedies...)

Art won't be with us much longer. But it's
going to get higher and higher on its way out.
Music beyond Beethoven. An incredible time to
be alive. I realized on my last trip that Shakespeare (fellow Taurus) will soon be envious of me.

You should hear the Velvet Underground.

*

Stranger _In_ _A_ _Strange_ _Land_ is a drama in
five acts. The first act incorporates every other
novel Robert Heinlein ever wrote.

Correction: first two acts. And of course
when the book came out, science fiction fans objected that it should have ended on page 218.
They were (for the most part) secure in the
alternate world sf-reading had provided them.
Heinlein in particular made us feel at home in
a universe more appealing, more rational, more
exciting, more real than the one facing us out
on the street. And then suddenly, in 1961 (minus 9),
Heinlein had the gall to write a novel transcending
the book reality we'd come to feel was our home.
Naturally we shat all over him. And--again, not
surprisingly--Heinlein himself was upset about the
book...particularly the popular acclaim it eventually received. Heinlein is a Cancer, born July 7,
1907. Minus 63.

The thing that strikes me most, on picking
up _Stranger_ again, is how incredibly conscious the
writing is, from page one. (Personal note: I first
read _Stranger_ in May of -1, almost seven years
after I bought a copy of the paperback at the 20th
World Science Fiction Convention, in Chicago. For
seven years, my sf fan's inbred snobbishness kept me
from reading my favorite writer's finest work.)
Heinlein spent a long time preparing for this book.
When it came out, it was Clear.

Writing's an incredible process (aren't they all?). Heinlein, as an exceptional writer, enjoys a highly intimate & intense relationship with the act of putting words on paper. It isn't just a matter of thinking something up and writing it down. There's something going on between you at every moment.

Creative genius is worthless. You must have receptive genius too.

*

Try to feel what's happening. Reader, what kind of a stance am I taking towards you? Heinlein not interested in the reader, reader as raison d'etre is all, the relationship is between author and protagonist. Neither one is the reader. Either could be each other. Does the author get confused?

Well of course he does!

And by what?

You see, there's something out there.

*

take your scissors and cut out these words
it's all right now

1-15

I wish I could describe, really make you feel, Carol and I in bed in the morning, or Lark and Tom and I fucking each other in the red bus by the church that night. But I know I can't quite do it yet, not the way I want it, all flesh and touch and affection. I'd like to excite you, write so the blood flows to your center, make you come. If I could reach my hand to your crotch, moving fingers gentle on cunt or cock, loving, embracing, till we're out of control, hips now moving on their own and
oh lover here we go...

Woman, I want to meet and thrust and fill you utterly... Man, I don't know what to do but somehow we'll get there.

Now you touch me...

*

So much has happened since the trip, now a week ago tho I really have no sense of time any more, I'd like to tell you about it but first I have to take you on the trip & that'll probably take the rest of this book.

We took acid--Lark, Paul, Tom Judy--sometime very late in the evening, after Judy and I had the talk I requested on page 66. Two events in the past--she was raped, she had a nervous break-down--long buried she now knew she had to work through before she could go further; still she wanted to go back to the city, felt unwanted and I asked if she were still planning to take acid before going back, I wanted to listen & absorb & help and the acid would help her get to it, in other words we should trip together.

I have long loved Judy, Judy of Judy & Tom, but it's hard for two slow self-conscious bulls to get together, a funny kind of shy you know. We have yet to make love tho I think she's beau-tiful. Even saying I'd like to trip with her was difficult, Not to push anything.

She said, would you like to take that s̶h̶o̶w̶e̶r̶ acid now?
And actually I was very tired (loving Lark all the last night, and then Carolanne all morning...and we never did get that nap we'd planned) but you can't say no, & of course Tom & Lark not to be left out, one way or another...

List of Entwhistle Books

Mayor of Harlem   David Henderson (Dutton)
Pushing Upward   Paul Williams (Dutton)
no name yet   Raymond Mungo (Dutton)
How To Commit Revolution in Corporate America
                 G. William Domhoff
Some Chronological Tales from July 1968 to July 1969
                 Artie Ross
There Must Be Some Way Out of Here   (Dutton..?)

Time Between   Paul Williams & family

Confessions of a Crap Artist --Jack Isidore (of Seville, Calif)
                 Philip K. Dick

Caspar Journal   Arthur Fankuchen

Collected Writings   Chester Anderson

Moving Through Here   Don McNeill   (Knopf)

Autobiography of a World-Savior   Mel Lyman

other Entwhistle authors include Wayne McGuire,
Dale Lewis, David Cohen, Frank Herbert, Michael
Lydon, Ron Cobb, Bob Crumb, Chip Delany, Tom
Brown, Robert Novick, Van Dyke Parks, David
Hartwell, Brian Keating, Richard Lupoff, Wayne
Hansen, Linn House...

The printed word is alive and well.

Watch this space.

About something being out there, interaction between author and protagonist and where does it come from, consider this: At any given moment a person's personality is a conscious stance, an affirmation of certain assumptions, this is who I am even tho in a broader sense we are each capable of uncertainty about almoost everything, on a moment-to-moment basis we can't afford that uncertainty, constant questioning gets us nowhere so we assume whatever stance is most natural to us, to this individual with his particular physical/emotional make-up and past experience and in his particular place in space and time... we are the sum of where we are and where we've been (what we've done & what's been done to us) but only as a convenience, potentially we could be ANYTHING since we each at each moment have the entire reservoir of mankind's conciousness (our subconsciouses) to draw on... more particularly a person can be whatever the assumptions that he won't let go of allow him to be, which is often a lot more than he chooses to be, we limit ourselves out of lack of faith & for practical purposes, if a man were to let go ALL his assumptions and realize his potential to become anyone and anything a man can be, he would be a god but he would also be absolutely vulnerable since with no assumptions you won't last long in any kind of confrontation.

What I'm saying here is that we are each the visible tip of an iceberg, the same iceberg, collective unconscious indiviudal conscious, the individual by definition is that which is perceptibly separate from the whole, imagine a sphere like a planet with three billion surface mountains, small peaks, extensions of the sphere; and this planet covered with water, ocean out of which the mountains poke, three billion islands. Each island perceives itself as separate from the others, though they are all extensions of the planet, sisters under the skin.

The surface of the ocean is the line between conscious and unconscious, the dividing point between One and All. We must affirm & stay aware of, act out, our individuality in order not to be swallowed by the ocean, but it would be nice to also be aware of and make use of the incredible reservoir of energy/life that we are all connected to (and through).

Personality is a conscious stance (ruled by the moon). A person's likes and dislikes are part of his person-

ality, and they change by the day. Individuality is
a person's whole, ruled by the sun, let's say it's
defined by his awareness. If you are aware of yourself as the entire human race (or as all life on
Earth) then you ARE the entire human race, but only
if you're wholly aware, to be intellectually aware
of this, as I am, means nothing in terms of identity. If I could feel at this moment what every
creature on earth feels, perceive what we all perceive, know all that we know, I would be all of
us. I am not. Not in the sense of the word "I"
as it is commonly used/

But "I" as this one lonely mountaintop COULD
be all of us if only I could let go & at the same
time stay conscious so completely that my only assumptions would be ones the entire human race agrees
on. (Are there such things? You better believe it!)

One of the ways a good writer works (this isn't
necessarily what I do, but it's what Heinlein does
in Stranger) is he pits his author's personality a-
gainst another of his potential personalities, he
makes use of the incredible reservoir of awareness
his openness allows him and creates two separate individuals, "author" and "protagonist," thesis and
antithesis, and the ego-struggle between these two
is the plot of the book, in the best sense of "plot,"
it is the process which holds and fascinates the
reader and (if the book is successful) it inevitably
climaxes in synthesis, transcendence, higher (fuller)
awareness.

Stranger in a Strange Land is the story oof
Valentine Michael Smith swallowing Robert Heinlein.
It is an examination of a myth so thorough that it
BECOMES the myth. It is the story of Jesus Christ.

The afternoon before the trip, Carolanne and I
went into Homer's to buy some shortening for the
donuts. While Carol shopped, I glanced at a local
 (Santa Rosa?) newspaper. It told me that (according
to a nameless source who had known him) Charles
Manson, the man with hypnotic eyes, leader of the
bunch of hippies who allegedly murdered Sharon Tate
etc, had for several years been obsessed with one
book; he lived by it, believed himself to be acting
it out in some way... The book, Stranger in a Strange
Land, was of course not taken so seriously by most
of its young readers blah blah blah...

We bought the shortening and went home.

Maybe I should tell you more about Entwhistle
Books. Back in February of minus two, in New York
City, Joel Hack and Dave Hartwell and I had a talk
about book publishing and what we wanted to do. And
what it turned out we wanted to do was break out of
all the accepted forms and find more direct methods
of binding, editing, distributing, everything.
In particular modern methods of distribution (for
books, records, films, toothpaste, everything) seemed
the root of all evil. Our consumer goods economy is
based largely on the assumption that, within reason,
you can sell anything as long as it's well-advertised,
well-distributed, well-displayed. So demand is taken
care of at the ad agency, and supply is determined
by superpowerful distribution combines (who control
the racks, as it were) and asshole economics profes-
sors go right on drilling their students in the laws
of the classic free market as though this were still
1790. The trick is to keep the public so confused
with meaningless programmed lusts and lots of stuff
all around to buy (on credit) that no one ever does
discover what their **NEEDS** are, they just keep scratch-
ing that material itch and raising welts and feeling
miserable.
We need an economy that will adjust itself
to people, not adjust people to it.

Anyway we agreed that the time has come when we
can no longer participate in the old economy, it is
too destructive of human aspirations, too great a
threat to the survival of life on this planet. But
what could we do? Get guns and shoot people? That
didn't sound very useful or high, and anyway what we
wanted to do was publish books. So we agreed we had
to ourselves begin to replace the old forms with increasingly higher ones.

And we realized that it wasn't a matter of someone
figuring out how things should be as opposed to how
they are, it's a matter of letting what's right happen.
Which means, let it happen. Encourage natural change
wherever and whenever you see the opportunity. Don't
lend strength to the atrophying old forms; withdraw
from them, make it easier for the forces of the times
to disperse the unhealthy clotting.

We decided to get into organic book publishing.
You don't tell a seed what to do; you let it grow.
Make sure you plant it in an environment where things
can grow, is all; and do everything you can to help
the natural change happen.

Joel went back to LA and got together with Chester
Anderson and the rest may someday be history. We're
kind of slow, but believe me we're steady. The forces
of change are inexorable. You can get in on this thing.

No typewriter now.

World-saviour is just a gig.

This time around...
    there's a need for liberation
  Too many people with monkeys on
            their backs
      And only 'cause they're frightened
            to be monkeys

    Ook ook.

    Reduction of fear is the revolution.

Nothing can be done about ecology without
  the dissolution of the economy.
Stop spending earning money!

    This means you !!!

    I dunno if it means me, I wanna use money
            to help liberate land...

Staying with Michael at FJ's house in Berkeley, visited
Larry McCombs today, got some more xeroxing done; flying to
Boston tomorrow, appointment on Monday with Seymour ("Sam")
Lawrence. Publishing adventure. Carol trying to decide--
for several days now--whether to go with me or back to Cal-
adan. She's afraid of the airplane ride.

        I realize I'm going to be forced to become a
            much better writer...this is an essay and
          there are some (maybe including me) who have
              trouble with the pace of certain thought-patterns
      And yet aesthetically I dig the patterns
                        I would like my music
            faintly to echo Emerson's
                        but our minds are a-jangle

            we can't read

            we can't read

        is doesn't make any sense, I can't think
                that carefully
                            I can't write

        only spit thoughts at you is all
            & try to say what happened

                    and that isn't enough
            nothing's enough until we love each other
    I have to become a better writer because I want to
        communicate
                with the people who read essays
                & the people who read science fiction
                & the people who don't read at all and
                    even those who don't listen to rock
                'n' roll   cause I'm all of these people
            and I'm trying to get it together

        The city is making me schizoid.
                Michael reads Dickens & <u>Huckleberry Finn</u>.
                Some people read newspapers.
                    I wish I were more interesting than a newspaper.
            it's not easy...
                Phil Dick novels really interest me, once
        I get going they really hold my attention
                that's very high praise
            few movies can hold me for five minutes
            ladies & trees fascinate me

                    fucking under redwoods is nice...

But what happened to the story? It's over, man, for this
book anyway, it's sleeping--
           Carol and I are in Berkeley, going to Boston to
       get a bunch of books published, New York, Arkansas
          Lark & Tom & Judy, Alan & Tami, Thistle, Yarrow,
          Raven Aeko Carl the Scotts 'n' evrybody Kay 'n' Ron
                              back in Mendocino
            probably, Andy & Judy in San Francisco maybe but
            I don't know where anyone is, I'm not there now
         I'll bet a lot of stuff is happening, especially, well
          especially with everybody and for all I know some
          of it's even being written down
                                    but not here; not now

                    y'have to stop somewhere
                    and try to catch up with yrself

          I have to. This is it. Here we are.

                  Makes me schizoid, 'cause meanwhile the
        present goes on...

                  I can't write about the past. Well, I remember
       I was sick as the acid started to come on, shitting my in-
       sides out but painfully slowly happens now and then,
       first time it ever happened to me on acid, made it easier
       in some ways, harder in others
                              you know how it is

         so I wasn't paying attention much to xxxxxxxxxxxxx
              what was happening with Lark or Tom or Judy
              Carolanne some and we made our peace
           mostly I was just sitting theretrying to get the pain out
                  naked on the john, tense
           and then it was okay
                  and I was really getting stoned, rushes, scary
              incredible and over to our house Lark alone playing
        "My Generation" very loud   she looked like a
                  very violent madwoman I realized the music can
         make you make those faces, bathed in the energy
                  but she scared me a little and I was worried she
                  really scared Judy
                              tho I don't know; overempathizing
           I guess   I don't know   acid rushing on

         I remember eventually we were all together
                    rapping this way and that

             Carolanne is trying to distract me
             I really don't want to write about all this

                    thank you Carolanne...

we're going to go to sleep soon

This is really an essay about Robert Heinlein, I
think he decided to do an Albert Schweitzer, you know,
really explore this Jesus thing
                            rationally, I mean
what would it really be like if a man
            possessing full knowledge of his godhood,
   that is, manhood   and sincerely wanting to
just help people be what they want to be, believe they want to be
   --postulate a mythically equivalent situation in
      our near future, create the situation and try to see
      what would happen
                        what would this naive & arrogant
         that is, unassuming & aware
            person do   what would happen?

So Heinlein thinks up an earthchild raised on Mars by
   the ancient & wise Martians, unspoiled product of a
higher culture, higher consciousness education training
   but since he's only an earthman, no more than an
      earthman   could be
                        can be
      he's the messiah, avatar, not do what I say but
               be like me

   And Heinlein has no love for messiahs
            not many thinkers do, in our western culture
      tho he recognizes the need

   just as he recognizes the need for authority and anarchy
         tho he can tolerate neither

                  we most of us know too much for our own
                                    life-styles

   so Heinlein gives birth to Valentine Michael Smith
         into a civilization Heinlein loves but can't respect
and a dynamic situation ensues

         Heinlein, I must make clear at this point, is an
      author who plays by the rules
                              of the universe he's created
   in fact he's helped make science fiction
      what it partly is: a literature in which an author
      tries to deal consistently with a world he himself has
      created... so altho Heinlein clearly dislikes Michael
   Valentine Smith, he can't put him down for being what he's
supposed to be   that's the rules   but the minute
   he steps out of line, you know the creator will pounce
         he doesn't like this punk kid
         arrogant   but naive, so you can't really get angry
   but you want to...

            you can hear the resentment in Heinlein's/Ben Caxton's
      voice. But Ben is just young Heinlein, the 1940
   good guy reporter, you'll find him in many early stories
      ("Our Fair City" comes to mind) yes surely Ben Caxton

is, consciously or not, RAH as a young man, and he
  (narrator of the fourth act; you can feel the pressure of approaching
 denouement--clearly expected by the author, but it never comes)
definitely resents Michael & absolutely mistrusts the entire
messiah trip   after all, he's getting all the girls
     and then there's Jubal Harshaw, Heinlein as an old, successful
  wise witty & lazy/energetic writer
                                   who likes Michael but is
     wisely cynical
                  I was young once
        but the joke's on him...

remember, if Ben and Jubal are Heinlein,
    Michael is Heinlein too
 but who among us wants to face up to that in ourselves?
 Heinlein doesn't, but the book runs away with him
        he's consistent to the end, tho it means ego-death

   son devours father

              the myths go on, but time changes the plots

            This is the Aquarian Age, Arien Jews didn't
       recognize the Piscean messiah and what can
                you expect from Christians/Pisceans now?

 Which is to say: Mel Lyman is Jesus Christ, or: V.M.Smith is
 jesus christ or somebody is, I mean it's happening again...

     transcendence

                        (a powerful myth's an oracle:
                            it announces the moment)

Now in Boston. Back to electric, Smith-Corona--recognize
the typeface? I've decided I want the "published book" of
Time Between to be a printed copy of this manuscript--if
that isn't what you're looking at there's been a slip twixt
lip & cup again... actually this typeface is funny, not the
same as the first part of this book which was mostly done
on an SC portable--Lark's--after the i's started jumping on
my machine, if you can remember that. My machine being the
one I traded with the school for my own SC elctr portable,
because the school's monster cut better stencils, which was
what I needed that day; now I have to trade in whatever's
around for a manual, no electricity in BC, should I get a
portable? Enough of this...

Carolanne decided to come, survived the flight, we're both
in Cambridge at my mother's apartment.

What I can remember of the early part of the trip is that
Judy & Tom seemed to have vanished, I thought Judy was frightened,
I thought they'd gone in a car to the school and was very
concerned because cars aren't safe and because they'd left
us   well they turned up   just went for a walk, everything's
ok, what's happening? no one knows. talking but not saying
anything, at least I can't remember it and occasionally Judy
wd say something like "this is like a doctor's office" fear
of the analytical, fear of turning everything to mud with our
minds and also fear of psychoanalysis because (I think) you
might be put away, locked up, you're crazy we've got you now
Judy's fear or my projection, certainly my fear some years ago,
haven't thought of it much lately, started affirming my craziness
in minus four and that's given me a kind of certainty, sanity,
no more duality I know who I am
                              sanity is the ability to swim
used to hate myself for my analytical mind, that's what I suddenly
remembered tripping with Judy (also Taurus), four years ago
I was so alone no lover and everything crumbling around me and
I really knew it was because I thought so much about things, used
to quote Cummings "since feeling is first who pays any attention
to the syntax of things can never wholly kiss you" and hated
myself for being me & making me lonely, would have much rather
been someone else and in love   or at least not alone

     hating myself for my loneliness, I'm not goingto do that again

but I understand, I empathize, with that fear of the analytical
          now I know how to get around my mind, which also
          enables me to use it
          and I'm not afraid of being crazy or being thought crazy or caught
                                                            crazy
ever since I decided I _was_ crazy & wanted to be & let that be my strength

          and now a new stage, because as I raved manic on that
     acid trip I realized my supreme arrogance
                              is that I believe myself sane

          we've become the reality, & overtaken the laws of chance

          I'm tired of dating these entries.
                              Tear down the walls!

Good meeting with Seymour Lawrence today, left him Time Between
up to the page before this, the Woodstock essay from Gathering
Together, Artie's book, Phil's book and Arthur's book...
   hope he likes them. Would like to work with him. He seems very
straight, by which I mean direct, a person who knows who he is,
you can work with him, not only likable but also no bullshit.
 We'll see.
          Dutton I'm unhappy with, they've had Pushing Upward
since June and still no galleys, I have to go to NY and get
that straightened out...I may have to type the book myself, can't
wait because once it's in type only then can I design it, decide
where to put Dale's drawings, white space etc. And this is my last
trip east for many months. Also Hal is holding up the checks for
There Must Be Some Way Out Of Here authors until he has a chance
to read and approve the manuscripts, and he's had some of them
for three months...all systems clogged...don't want to burden
Dutton with new books when they're too busy to take care of the
ones I've given them. But otherwise I'm happy with them, probably we can work it out tho it won't be painless... I also
don't like Hal's apparent attitude towards Dale's drawings,
a million dollars they've made from Winnie the Pooh and now they
won't allow bears on the cover of my book! child-like stuff a
threat to someone's manhood. This is silly. Do I have time to play
these games?
          But I love the people involved, if they'll either
face me down or get out of my way I know we can work things out.

   How soon can I finish this book? Well, I have to tell you
about world saviours, why is a raven like a writing-desk, make
clearer this bit about R. Heinlein being swallowed by his own
creation and what sort of myths are we dealing with here anyway?
In fact, towards the end (near sleep) of that acid trip lying
in bed with Carolanne and Tom between us I realized we are ready
now to act out any myths we want, any at all, we should just
choose which ones appeal to us and avoid the bummers, what the
hell, but our life-acting is now not just role-playing but myth-
enactment, which means we each epitomize & contain the human race
and are ready to perform perfect dramas scripted by and for the
collective unconscious itself. I mean all myths of brothers, lovers,
                                  demons
saviours, skeptics, heroes, cowards and saints, all literature,
all history, it's going fast and on its way out more available than
                           with
ever, ours to play around going out of consciousness sale
               everybody's gotto
          go

               FaustHamletOedipusChristBuddhaAhabHelen
          onyourmarkgetreadygetset
          go

                              go!

hurry up please it's time

relax.

hurry up please it's time

       don't push me, dammit

hurry up please

              I don't want to get heavy with anybody, my job isn't to push
          it's to pull seduction don't you want to live with me?
                     seduction and when you do give in, you discover it's okay
                  it's nice

           feels good to breathe fresh air
               fuck many people
            be able to say what you feel
               not carry money
         nice to know you really are a part of things
             not to be afraid   you'll make a fool of yourself
               nice to be a fool
         when you know they laugh & fear because you're free
                 and you know you're not going to hurt anybody
         not to carry a gun
                 not to cling to the railing
               'cause you're sure of foot
           and sure of each other
                 not to doubt your brother
               'cause why would he hurt you?
               he'd have to be crazy   (since he'd feel it too)
                 and that's behind us now

        nice to know that there's room
             'cause we know what we need
                 and we know how to get it:
            by not wanting more

            we're making <u>progress</u>!

                   minus five: I Can't Get No Satisfaction
              year one: ...you get what you need...

         not that the Stones have learned better, which is true, but that
            times have actually changed, they speak for us all you know

               if you try sometime
               you justmight find
                   you get what you need...

     (and if you want it baby
      you can come all over me)

and time between is transition, not there yet, no longer there
                                                        here
          just here is all and it's part of the experience of the times
  the pain of transition
        common to our parents, our children & us
     not getting to keep what we've had, never quite reaching what we
                                              strive towards
    we are very old
                  two thousand years old, an era, as old as you can be
       and very young
                  year one young
                           young as the new age
 the Caesars height of the Roman empire peak of the Arien age
      and even as it climaxed the Piscean messiah
            was somewhere being born
    and the glory that was Rome could not o'ershadow him, nor long
  contain the energy released
                           when the moment is highest it's over
        be not sad   be like the sun at midday
            Christ is born
            ally ally in free

time between, don't you feel it? we were not born Aquarians
      maybe our children, or our children's children
      will never know other than the higher consciousness
      we only can glimpse coming down over the trees
            I wan' it I wan' it I wan' it
                you can't have it   !

      okay, okay I'll cling to what I have
      sorry, this universe is being repossessed

            the only pain is separation &
            the only joy is breakthru

      These really are difficult times to live in.
  They really are exciting times, fantastic times, the truth is
     I'm very glad I'm here   it has its points

            I want you
            because time is on his side
            I want you

            open to me my sister

for two weeks almost I've been living in a fantastic world
as though I'd been eating opium
I'm very nearsighted, 20/200 I think and for a dozen years
or more I've worn my glasses all my waking walking hours
taking them off to sleep or make love
and then one fine acid trip at the other end of the bed
from Judy Aeko Lark & Tom
off they fell and I abandoned them
escaping out the window
Tom brought them later I knew he would I love him
but I'd already left them behind
and everything's so natural now, no focus but no headaches
because I haven't been straining, I don't really want to see
hard edges; whatever I do see I'll accept
it's my reality anyway, why should I worry what I don't see
isn't there
after a while I'll learn to read minds a different way
since I can't see eyes and faces
maybe the movements of head and hands, maybe the aura
I'll compensate
I don't drive so that's no hassle
I've actually been reading more since I quit them
I'm interested in doing exercises, I'll improve my sight as
much as I can but I'm not counting on anything
I'm pretty happy
and very free

and anyway, I was saying the world is so fantastic
lights and colors   fuzzy like blue haze around the moon
soft reasonable
people more real when they are more close
girl-watching a problem but I can just get closer
compensation
take off my glasses; as tho now I am always making love to everyone
and it feels different, the medium around me
is more sensuous, more personal, & tho I act fuzzy
I'm slowly learning to pay attention

whatever sense perceptions I receive I'll construct my reality out of
kind of nice to get a whole new set at this late stage
lots of acid leaves me flexible

and maybe I'll go back to the glasses, but from now on I'll know I don't
        have to
liberation
and maybe I won't want to
I don't want to now

it's a strange new world & not too secure & I love it

words keep tumbling out. Charles Manson. Where does he fit in?
A lot of people talking about him; not much said. Demon hippie.
In the supermarket people look at you a certain way, it's okay,
I understand, all hippies look like Manson to me too   and it's
funny,people aren't frightened, they're curious
             I'm curious
Manson seems to me if what is said is true (and if not it's
myth now anyway) he has a certain kind of power
 we've all suspected exists but are surprised to find in this reality
a strength I should say, and yr strength becomes power if
    others are weak & frightened of yr strength
  tho that doesn't seem to be what was happening exactly
girls & men not frightened but respectful
Manson more real to them than anyone else so why not
                                        do what he says
better to do what Nixon says?
                       we do you know
better to follow orders shoot the women & babies?
of course Manson murders (alleged) no more acceptable than Song My
         but what are you going to do about it?
                more cops?

         more consciousness

it's the only way out, you know it, you <u>know</u> it...
but it's asking a lot, it means you're responsible
<u>not</u> guilty
<u>responsible</u>
no one else is going to do anything, it's up to you
when Charles Manson tells you to kill someone what are you going to do?
kill him?
say no? right to his face? to those eyes, those "eyes whose irises
seemed on the trembling point of spinning like wheels" (Theodore
Sturgeon, <u>More than Human</u>)?
brother, you gotta be <u>strong</u> to do that.
a cop-out would be to sort of decide that it wasn't such a bad thing
        to do, really
 those people pigs anyway
  come back as something better next time
  after all, no moral code to fall back on
  Richard Nixon took care of that Catholic church took care of that
  mother and father took care of that corporate ameriea took care of that

so with no moral code & not as much strength as C.M. you just might
           say okay
            why not?
      shoot some smack, they lied to you about marijuana
      kill a cop, they say it's okay for viet-c.
   if you can kill anyone, you can kill anyone
     U.S. morality says you can kill some people
        might as well be who Charlie says
           he's your friend

And from the acid trip page 67 I remember just sitting there screaming
very calm & manic rapping away
can't breathe the air and we keep pouring more poison into it why?
same reason people smoke cigarettes, why do you keep smoking cigarettes?
don't you care if you poison yourself, isn't it contradictory yes but
I can't I can't
YOU CAN'T?? And you have the nerve to rap at me about revolution,
up against the wall motherfucker, capitalist imperialist bullshit
and power to the people? Ecology? How you gonna live in tune with the
ecosystem of the whole planet even once you know how if you can't even
keep from posioning yourself??
                    that kind of talk too heavy for most friends
          prefer revolution bullshit
            but I only ask the questions cause there are answers
              I don't rip cigarettes from people's mouths, try to
                  make you feel uncomfortable, this isn't a moralistic trip
            just want to ask you, so you'll tell me (can't really ask
              myself 'cause I don't smoke)
                              how can you keep doing it?
            find out how, why, then maybe find out what has to be
          changed to get you free of this, should be a good clue how
            to get us all free
                        of our collective neuroses
                NEUROSIS! What stupidity! simpering cowardly nervous
          disorder caused by the culture but accepted thru fear of the culture
            why not go psychotic and get it out of your system?
            what are you waiting for?
          if the culture makes you crazy only way to destroy the culture
              is to act sane
            anything else is supporting it
              act SANE
              real sane, not culture-accepted standards
                        what makes sense to you
                Stop being afraid of being crazy
        people who smoke cigarettes are crazy
                as Crazy as Manson, he's not trying to kill himself
          you're crazy!
                  go sane

          screaming or anyway rapping very loud but feeling good, rapping
    about stranger in a strange land, Heinlein too attached to this culture
      to accept his own rational rejection of it, prefers to lose faith
    in himself: oh well, just a science fiction story, why are you kids
                taking it so seriously?
          so many of my friends
              choose to doubt themselves rather than admit
              they smoke cigarettes because of tv commericals
            smoke cigarettes because they're Americans
              like to drive cars 'cause of neurotic programming
          maybe even like to kill people, it's okay: Bonnie & Clyde
              man, Bonnie & Clyde were heroes!
            Charles Manson, Sirhan Sirhan heroes but
                we have to be greater heroes than them!!
              our moral code demands it
          we have to cut through the gordian knot of The System
            without murdering each other
                    and we can
                      so stop acting crazy

This means you, Weathermen, fucking romantic intellecutals
        stop acting crazy, that's for the old world
        driven insane by tv and lying economists
                    who pretended they knew what was happening
        driven insane by man vs. life propaganda
                    conquer outer space
                triumph over nature   beat back the elements
    driven crazy through church-endorsed fear of desire
                which is fear of need
        fear of their bodies
                        fear of their friends
            lists of what not to fuck
                lists of when not to fuck
            lists of how not to fuck
            crazycrazycrazyCRAZYYYYYYYYYYYYYYY

                            but that's not us.

        We don't have to play those games, I'm not afraid for my manhood,
    I look like a girl with my long hair and let boys I love hold my cock
    and read children's books and do what my women say
                    when it makes sense to me
            or I'm not feeling stubborn
                    and I know I'm a good lover
    but I believe
                everyone is
            we're not deranged Ernest Hemingways, no suicide necessary
        because it wasn't an act to begin with
                    so the show's never over
                not neurotic Norman Mailers, stabbing wives in public
                    but scared of masturbation

            when I was a kid I thought at least I'd be done with
                this damn shameful masturbating when I could get
                            fucked regularly
            and I'm only beginning to realize that it's a whole
        other thing
                    and I can fuck twice a day and still
                    want to be alone and jack off now and then

                because I'm not crazy;
                so I can say these things

                    don't have to kill my parents
            don't have to destroy U.S.A. 'cause I know it doesn't exist
                    anyone thinks it does is crazy

        true someone's killing the Panthers, makes me angry
                    & scared
                so we've got to stop that
    but I don't see how guns can stop that, don't see how atom bombs can
                    stop that

            don't need weathermen   just stick wet finger in air

        sanity the ability to swim
                    jump in the water if you don't know how
                and save yourself, you heroo

more? more? don't know what to say. I want to be clearer but haven't
got time, mind falling apart
                              on the trip I was clear, very clearly,
           but scary I guess
          got higher and higher (I'm not there yet) till I was saying
      everything, courage not to care if no one could stand the real me
         I held Mel's book & knew I had to be me even if that meant
       discovering myself alone
                    expecting to be alone, but not trying for it, just letting off
steam, saying it all, flipping out, going crazy for Judy cause she doesn't
dare but we're all the same person so I'll do it this time
               and looking around, I wasn't alone
               go back to page 49, read what Mel said
       you can see that alone would make sense
              but Carol still there, really not afraid of me
                   really not afraid of me! oh I love her
       and in the other room lying on his makeshift bed I thought I
    detected   quiet but he'd been there all along, Carol didn't even know it
                   Carl
              Carl and Carol not scared of me, I could flip out as much
                        as I want
                        not alone any more Mel, progress
          three of us
                   Carl knowing that loneliness too,
          sometimes he has to lose everyone else
                   to stay true to the land
              & does it because that's what you do
       we are all world-saviours when we dare to be ourselves
                   completely ourselves when that need is there and
                   damn the torpedoes
       Carl & Carol & Paul and now we were no longer in Mendocino, I
          suddenly remembered there was no decision to make I had already
    decided for British Columbia
                   and never left there, only returned to take care of
                        business
       Paul Williams, Refuge Cove, B.C. my address
                   and there I was, Lark & Tom & Judy not ready yet
                        scared off
                   but Carl and Carol right there, me there,
          fantastic sense of strength, warmth for all of us
       not as alone as we used to be, might still have to be
                   and we're ready, we can be, won't back down
              but from here we can only go forward, I was ready
       to make a stand under worse circumstances than it turned out
                   prevailed
                   so we know we can make it
          we'll make a stand in B.C.
              the forces of decay won't drive us back, for at last we know
       we're stronger than they are
                   and Lark & Tom & Judy and all will be with us soon,
          they have to do their trip till it reaches the point where we
       all coincide again and we have to do ours to catch up with them
              you're not always together but never apart
          this may not make much sense but at least it's down on paper,
maybe someday I can make it all clearer but the time for feeling
                                        is now

if you're scared of people you aren't on the other side yet
              stop being scared of people & join us in paradise
                   we'll try to scare you away but we won't succeed   (?)
          don't you want to live with me?

                    Aquarius/Leo
                         year one...

"I've got to check my stove,"
he said, and it's winter in
Massachusetts, full moon out
in the country, sky over snow.

minus four degrees.

many fine dogs and people.

talk of money and cars, rip-offs
and misadventures. good sense
of humor. little talk of family
or coming together but that's
what's happening and it's good
to see.

huddling around the stoves.

     "When's the last time
you watched the news in color?"

swallowing the roach.

I'm writing in a notebook,
between small lines, slows
me down. Which is probably
a good idea, but I don't know.
                Time Between.
 What I feel about Heinlein
is that he is not a writer who
figures it all out in advance.
How he writes--like how I'm
writing this is I have a sense
of what it feels like up to
here, so I'm kind of obligated
to write only in a way that
feels good in terms of the
context, on some intuitive
level I have to keep the flow
going; and I have in my head
certain associated topics of
conversation that I want to
express myself on before the
book is over (so I keep coming
back to Jagger, Manson, Heinlein, the acid trip etc); and
that stuff plus what is or has
been happening around (and to)
me plus the way I feel at the
moment is the barrel I dip into
as I sit here writing.
 And how Heinlein writes is he
thinks up a situation, a dynamic situation y'know so something has to happen, but it's
not obvious what... and then he
has to write, he's got his
characters and his world and a
barrelful of exposition and
funny incidents, clever lines
to dip into as he goes along,
the only question is what's going to happen, and being a rational (and imaginative) man
he looks at the situation and
eventually sees only one thing *that*
can happen... y'dig? In a
sense the situation, once arrived at, stumbled into, writes
its own plot, it determines the
events rising out of it, in
collaboration with the author.
A different author faced with

the same situation--Heinlein
once gave Ted Sturgeon a double-
handful of plot-starters, to
help him out of a dry spell--
would write a different story,
would see other imperatives.
It's like throwing the I Ching--
hell, a given reading is different not only for each reader but
for each different moment in the
reader's life. Still, the reader
doesn't invent the reading--he
feels he's getting it from the
Ching. A collaboration.
  Heinlein, I am convinced, es-
sentially wrote Stranger in a
Strange Land from the premise,
in collab. w/the premise, that
an extremely potent (self-aware)
human being who is by upbringing
completely ignorant of human
culture, mores, civilization,
assumptions arrives on the scene
and feels a need to better the
lot of his fellow-creatures, a
sincere desire to help them a-
chieve what they say they want,
which is basically his natural
state of happiness, realization
of the human potential, the Garden of Eden. A messiah. Powerful, innocent, sincere. Given a
man strong enough to bring it
off, sincere and innocent enough
not to doubt himself, what would
happen? Heinlein uses his imagination to create the situation:
a human child, of extremely
well-selected stock, is born on
Mars as a result of the first,
abortive, mission to that planet. He is raised as a Martian by
the Martians, who are clever
buggers, being pretty old. He
never encounters the possibility
that he might not be able to
learn to slow down his metabol-
ism, use his innate psychic powers, etc, so with good training
he learns to do these things
very well. He is raised in a
Martian culture, an older and
far saner (says who? the author?
this reader, at least, feels
it's saner, and suspects that's
what the author intended--for

plot purposes, of course) civilization, in which the individual
is aware that he not only repre-
sents, he is, the divine power,
comprehends his life (and therefore death) as part of the large
cycle that is the health of the
whole organism, the Martian
race, all life on the planet.
Etc, etc. There is a non-genetic
family relationship based on affection and codified (made sacred) by ritual, the sharing of
water (a precious substance on
a dry planet--which fact was also central to another great 60's
novel, Dune--wonder what the
collective unconscious is trying
to tell us...?)
    ...Anyway, Valentine Michael
Smith arrives on Earth, brought
back by the 2nd Mars Expedition,
naive and (in Earth & Heinlein's
eyes) arrogant, and the fun begins. Heinlein sets that up, and
sets up the Earth V.M.S. arrives
into (remarkably like our own,
though set in a future where the
Pill is advertised on tv and the
Boss is the U.N. Sec-General and
the characters are transplants
from 1941. The story takes place
in plus thirty-five, more or
less; but like all good science
fiction it really takes place in
(what the author perceives of)
the present). There are a few
hundred pages in which Michael
as a character is well in the
background, as Ben Caxton, com-
petent young reporter, Jill
Boardman, pretty nurse, and Jubal Harshaw, super-competent old
writer, free Michael from the
iron grip of the central government and in the process acquire
an incredible amount of capital
and political power and in general have a good time snubbing
established authority. This is a

familiar theme in Heinlein's novels. He's always either advocating authoritarianism or writing heroic--and thoroughly delightful; I love the first 2 acts of _Stranger_--tales of a few men overthrowing Authority. Must have been something between him and his father.

This first part of the book is pretty much under Heinlein's control. It's damn well written, a good indication that it wasn't thoroughly thought out (which tends to deaden a novel's spirit), but Heinlein characters, like Houdini, have fought and slipped out of so many fascist bureaucratic traps that it's second nature now. R.A.H. certainly projects no real doubt about the eventual success of Ben & Jill & Jubal vs. Amerika (er, I mean, the Federation).

Then part three. Michael sets out in the world, to learn the ropes. In the first two books we, the readers, got to know Michael, Jill, Ben and Jubal and the secretary-general and the girls. In the third book we begin to know that same world, these people, through Michael's eyes. He begins to know us. Things are getting higher.

Another day, another typewriter. This one's an Underwood,
manual ancient and it feels pretty groovy. Everyone here
(at this western Mass farm) is restless, Steve wants to
go to the city/doesn't want to go to the city, nothing to
do I guess, I mean that stage where there are things to do
but you don't want to do any of 'em, too much of a transition getting into 'em, but you want to do something so
you hang around doing nothing, feeling loose but frustrated.

Called Carolanne, she stayed in Boston, I've been gone
two days, yesterday she freaked out and went to a hospital
so she could talk to a doctor, today she sounds fine, together in her head, doesn't bother me, I know it's just
letting off steam (not sure what she does when she "freaks
out"; in our five months together this is the first time
she's done it) and I kind of had a feeling she was waiting,
unconsciously, till I wasn't around... She's told me she gets
hysterical, then I noticed that she never did tho the opportunity had arisen more than once; so I kinda assume that her
subconscious sees no percentage in freaking with me around...
so what the hell, I don't worry about it. We're making real
progress, both of us, and I just wish I could get her off
tranquilizers completely (she's cut down a lot). But they're
no worse than cigarettes; I guess we get our friends off
their dependencies by seeing to it that they have no <u>need</u>
for dependencies, get 'em so high all the time that sticking
a cigarette in one's mouth would seem to them like sucking
off a carburetor. I'll probably go back to Boston tomorrow
if anyone's driving from one of the farms out there; but
Carolanne's fine, just riding the roller coaster, we all do
and if we can get help we scream for it but if we can't we
just ride it out, often it's good to get it over with. Some
people need to cry themselves out once a week; they should
be encouraged. I'm not very depressive, myself; don't know
why or how but I'm sure I compensate for it in some other way.

Heard the bootleg live Stones album last night, illegal recording of their Oakland concert, <u>fantastic</u> music, "I'm Free"
like a fist through a window the whole aesthetic different
because Jagger too hoarse, too immediate to be sinuous, instead a pure energy riff, some genius perceptions tho you might
think at first you don't like these versions of familiar
songs as well soon you're overcome by something that is happening on an even heavier level than the carefully-recorded
Stones music, this stuff is all even fours and tour de force,
repetition strength and clarity everything so clear you can't
even recognize it, I mean it's just <u>there</u> with no context, no
explanation possible, cutting through to reality. Keith Richards
incredible musician by all standards, Robert Johnson, Beethoven,
Jagger our screaming subconscious screaming for all of us like
me on that acid trip.

this lp a fantastic painting or movie
blam blam blam boogahhhhhhhhhhhhhhhhhhhh

        Okay baby, let's bring it on home.

Why write books? Well, I'm feeling better about it everyday,
records have a real place in this transitional world we live
in and books do too, people here who don't read ~~really~~ have
been reading my Woodstock piece and liking it and so that's
really satisfying, like they only don't read the way in -10
you might not have listened to music much, just because nothing
really fantastic or alive was happening in the present, some
fantastic art left over from the past as always, don't knock
it, Moby Dick or Beethoven can really flip you out, but there
is also the thing of particpating in something happening now
and most people have an aesthetic of the printed word that
makes it almost impossible to write what they want to say, because of the distance you know, they have to figure out a
clever framework in which to tell a particular sotry a certain
way that will make the right point and think all this out in
advance, that isn't the way rock music works or this new music
that's coming in now that's even better than rock because it's
completely of the moment, the Avatar record offers clues to
that, also the Airplane lp because they've left their individual and group egos behind, a bunch of people find themselves
in the same room and start beating drums, fucking, screaming
till the room sounds just like the people in it, that's music,
we want to be OPENED. Well, and I think there's a new sort
of word-use that's beginning that will bring people back to
books, some people, the way rock brought people to music, actually "books" are unnecessary we can do it with bards and
xerox machines, but like I want to and feel I'm beginning to
put on paper my actual consciousness, or somebody's, the way
a rock song has all the enrgy of what three minutes can be,
forcing us to desire and lead fuller lives, longer minutes,
which is now happening, in general I think music gives people
energy, books can give them strength and the other way around
sometimes of course and there's also awareness which all the
arts provide, watching tv after awhile is like taking acid
because the information overload breaks down neural formations
in the brain, assumptions are lost as the canals overflow and
the old categories channels become flooded and run together,
a period of confusion and then new assumptions, new riverbeds,
emerge, the waters recede a little, the excretion system in
the brain starts working again and with your new assumptions
you're more able to pass completely on certain kinds of low-con-
sciousness information, leaving room in the files for the higher
awareness stuff, acid achieves this breakdown and spring house-
cleaning by triggering a chemical reaction, tv etc, the modern
world, causes a more gradual erosion of thought-patterns, sometimes reaching critical mass in the form of nervous breakdown or
schizophrenic break but just keep going you always come out the
other side in a world more intuitively rational than the one
you'd been trying to pretend was real. Imagine people buying
life insurance! It's incredible. No wonder the life insurance
companies send their police after LSD. They should pull out
the tv plugs too. That may look like total bullshit harmless
that's going out over the tube but there's so much of it that
it causes consciousness transcendence breakthru anyway. All
systems breaking down. Organic forms, green life grows out of
   the rubble.

The more it snows, tiddley-pom...

Sirhan Sirhan. I was always fascinated with this man. Didn't
know why at first, something in his eyes, the conviction in his
face, didn't look like frightened, fucked up mad dog Oswald,
looked like a man who knew what he was doing, very young, his
thin hands clasping each other it would always say in the papers,
his early faith in his lawyers, his disillusionment, his willingness to affirm what he'd done, so rare in America, his lack
of unnecessary arrogance or pride, only when someone "lied"
about _him_, doubted him or tried to confuse others, did he speak
out desperately, arrogantly, assert his sanity and his faith in
himself. The photo of him in Life Magazine was on my wall for
a long time, no on the door to the bathroom actually, intense,
staring, people wouldn't recognize him, ask: who's that? Sirhan
and the picture of Mel were too heavy for Nancy Magic when she stayed
in my house, she had to take them down till I got back, and it
wasn't that I appreciated Kennedy's death or anything weird like
that, actually I liked him, wanted to see him President (though
anyone's okay; I'm really happy with Nixon), and when I think of
Sirhan Sirhan as the murderer of a man, flesh & blood RFK bleeding
out his life on the ballroom floor, gunshots, I can't affirm that
under any circumstances, men should not be murdered, we must not
be murderers. But Sirhan to me is a hero, too, one of the great
heroes of the 20th century, a man who cut the Gordian knot, shot
through umpteen levels of newspaper padding and media myth reality, "democracy" in which 200 million people (actually several
billion affected by U.S. actions) supposedly govern themselves
like so many thousands did in Athens. Sirhan fired the shot
heard round the world in the war for individual freedom, shot a-
nother individual who had willfully made himself a target and
donned the false cloak of corporate immortality, jets in the
Jordanian sky sure I'll vote for that get the Jewish vote it's
what the people want, one man jerking off making these decisions,
a hundred men, pretending to be a hundred million but it's media
fantasy lies, Sirhan played the game on Kennedy's terms, okay
you want to say for the sake of Jewish votes you put those
bombers American superweapons we cannot hope to fight in my
people's sky, you put it there? I believe you RFK I love you
I embrace your reality I am a simple man who believes what the
media says, it is real and you did it and I love you but I must
shoot you you are killing my people _you_ you you you are the
target, you wish to be more than a man, be the embodiment of
a million men, you must accept the karma of this mass of men,
maybe I can talk to you, convince you, pull out the jets, do
not kill our people, no, no there is no hope I have been betrayed
Senator Kennedy I love you but you are at war with my people
it is not the Israelis without your money, your jets, they are
nothing, we are who we've always been, you are the enemy, you
are the target I hate you lover you've betrayed my trust I love
you die die this is not crazy it is sane it is sane if a man
paints a target on himself and acts with the arrogance and power
of a million and causes death and misery at the same time he
strives for a better world, is it not right to shoot at such a
target? If it is right for America to sell weapons of death to
our enemies, to kill and assassinate in Vietnam, if there is
ever righteous murder is this not it? I don't know, I don't know
it's hard to make up my mind, I will go down to the hotel, maybe
I can talk to him no he thinks only of his success he even forgets he has ever signed death warrants...   I shoot you RFK.

RFK must die...   Sirhan was right. If any murders are
righteous--and I believe none are--then the murder of Robert
Kennedy by this particular man Sirhan Sirhan was without
question righteous, America must end all it's killing all all
before it can begin to consider Sirhan a murderer he is more
a world-saviour, the trap was closing, slow inexorable, the noose
around our necks, corporate state, the people contained by fear
and avarice, the power growing mightier and mightier and when
the last brick is in place no individual will be able to challenge us ever again. Us? who is us? Who is US? Not a man, no
men, you are all but puny men, I am the STATE I am the light
natural descendant of USA Catholic Church General Motors CBS
Bell Telephone CPSU all institutions ever now met and joined
as ONE institution we did it we met and joined before the
people could, come together, the state monolithic now... But
as the contracts are being drawn up and shivering humanity
ready to sign, anything, anything, I'm so scared a shot rings
out the golden boy falls quick get the other golden boy
he's not ready the people are uneasy a fat bald man comes out
from the back room "An accident, an agitator, he'll be okay
in the morning you can come back and sign the paper then" but
the individual is shocked, confused, okay in the morning? but
he saw him bleeding to death before him, there on the tv, there
with the contract about to be signed who could have done this
foul deed? how could they let it happen? no hate but confusion,
stunned even beyond fear, catatonia he doesn't show up in the
morning to sign the contract curses, foiled again
                          the corporate state crumbles

        Sirhan Sirhan you thin young man intense courageous mad as
a hatter, you saved us all, you and everyone who has remained
convinced of his potency in the face of the apparent invinci-
bility of the technological state. we vote with our lives, most
of us are afraid to vote scared to death sheep we are herded
therefore a few of us are heroes act out our convictions
crazy or not affirm our own world-view, our sanity Rafael M.
another hero, hijacked a jet plane from San Francisco to Rome,
I'm a man, I'm more real than all these jets and nations. They
loved him in Italy, I love you Rafael, my heart is with you
Sirhanyou men have courage, you are not intimidated you bring
us back from the brink of being swallowed & incoporated into
the state Buckmister Fuller technological world-brain fascism
program the machine to know who the poeple are and take care of
their needs jets are for people with money money is for those
who play ball with the system jets are for people with power
power is having pretty hair and lots of money and some votes
okay clean Gene I'll take over here   they won't vote for you
you know this is a democracy that means you have to give way
to whoever can attract good Neilsen ratings Bobby is here
Bobby is dead died in a war in a foreign country probably
didn't even know he was in that war, who can keep track of these
things, 50 jet fighters? Sure. That's what the people want, Jim?
That's what they want,boss. Okay okay. Now about this primary...
Poor Bobby. A pawn himself, just an ambitious boy like so many rock
stars etc trying to get what Columbia Records said was rightfully
theirs, the Rolling Stones in Miami accepting those free Plymouths
because in America everything is free said Keith   sorry Keith
                                                  you're wrong

Approach to
The Power of the Great
(yesterday it was the p. of g.
to Marrying Maiden)

Interesting... "becoming great" is another name
for "approach"

the news from home (it's just a shot away):
Huckleberry saved from the knife...we had decided, with
misgivings, to have Huck spayed (Arthur left without giving
her away & Carol and I, the only real dog-lovers, are definitely leaving for B.C. about the time Huck'll have puppies)
...and now it develops that Bill Rickhardt will rent our
house (I didn't think the owner would rent it out again; he
wants to sell) and will take Huck and the puppies in the
bargain! So the lady has someone to take care of her now,
fate has acted to stop her hysterrectomy. God, the relationships between man and "domestic" animals are strange.

Lark spending most of her time with Tom & Judy; they've
all gotten together, which seemed to be what was happening
on that last acid trip, the perfect solution of course, and
they're at Bobbie's now, where there's a nice large bed.

Carl back to Canada; Ron was going to go with him but
didn't; everything fine. Alan maybe will go to Mexico when
I get back, to skin dive in warm water one last time. Andy
and Judy sounded well. Tami fine. Should have asked after
the babies and Strider and Moksha, but tlephone conversation
is always difficult, only a three-minute elation.
Through love and trust it's gonna work out fine...

I wish I was home. I'm glad I'm here. I'd like to be
with Carolanne right now--here would be a good place for
that. Nice to have a new lover for a night or two but she's
not a new love, I can't get to know her, even if she were
I'd be missing Carolanne; we sure have a good thing.

I'm on the edge of depression--of all things--just
   below threshold and it's bringing me down.
                  self-doubt
         I keep flashing on how great this book is,
   how much it does and is that nothing I've written
      has ever been before; but I'm also repeatedly reminded
of how unsatisfactory the book is
         how clumsy   it's all stops and starts
   mad raps that never quite climax, related stuff just
desperate to be brought together & higher but that's
         not quite   happening
         not yet   happening
            but I have to have faith in myself
      and I do, but like everyone else I'm embarassed at
   my ego   I hesitate to affirm my arrogance, I
know how often I know I'm right
                              and I'm wrong
      so I want to be careful & also be certain & brave
            and that pulls me in separate directions
   I was just saying to John
                  on the subject of our restlessness,
         Steve today so eager to get to the city,
            drawn like a magnet
            and yet longing to stay home
         just like me when I travel from Mendocino
   we have come to expect change, we need it
            two weeks without a blown mind   two days!
               and we start getting horny
            we want to rush into the future, we can't wait
      but all those security trips

            our aspirations are incredible
               our fears are great
                  these things pull at us
            tug-of-war

      Tom and Judy at the School, dynamic opposition

            Tom for pushing upward, Judy for holding together

   in a couple you can at least get it out in the open
                  that opposition is inside me now
            from within I am pulled apart

            we must break free of the city's gravity

in Mendocino we've more or less succeeded at that, except
that the call of adventure and the idea that that other place
can somehow fill our emptiness and stuff like my desire to
be published through the old forms
      for prestige and money mostly, ego-gratification
                  God, that's ridiculous!

         isn't it?

Cambridge   Jan 25

Dear Tom:

I love you and want to touch you. That's all I know.
The rest is confusion.

Our desires (our fears) are often programmed — not by
experience, but by the media, the people around us.

Our pleasures are real.

Pleasure is not the realization of desire. It is the
stimulation of our minds, our nervous systems, our hearts.

It takes place in the present.

People should give each other pleasure, when they can.
Giving pleasure is pleasure in itself; everyone gains.

Our fears and desires are what get in the way.

Webster's Dictionary of Piscean Age Assumptions and
Confusions defines "homosexual" as an adjective: "exhibiting sexual
desire toward a member of one's own sex."

What is sexual desire? Blood rushing to the cock?
Dollar bill to the newsboy for this month's Playboy? What is
"exhibiting sexual desire"? something different from acting it out?

Don't answer. The Piscean Age is behind us now. Our
Playboy subscriptions have all gone limp.

Love is where you find it.

Carol and I are here in Cambridge, listening to Creedence (Clearwater and the Poor Boys). I've just been out in the county for 3 days, at the formerly-LNS farm in Montague (western Mass.). Temperatures down to twenty below. Good things happening at the farm: but no kids, neither at Montague nor at Ray's place in Packer's Corner, Vermont (the two farms are as closely related as Calatan and the School, though maybe an hour apart). At Montague consciousness is still focused around Marshall Bloom's suicide, last November first. Not that everyone's down, they've gone beyond that, but Marshall's death is still the central fact that most (and almost can't) be dealt with. It's hard to explain. People don't sit around and argue about why he did it — I didn't hear a word of explanation or speculation my whole time there. But Verandah (from Packer's Corner) wears Marshall's dark covering robe always (and says she hasn't been cold since she put it on), Johnny Wilton's New Babylon Times features in its upcoming second issue poetry by Verandah, the first chapter of Steve Diamond's projected book on Montague, etc, all based around Marshall's death. Raymond's Occasional Drop centered on the subject (without really mentioning it), Steve M. is writing his experiences the day Marshall died and at the Sagittarian Bash (the other recent major event — an attempt at affirmation of life, a super mescaline party which apparently meant something different to each person there).

Death is a challenge to awareness that seemingly no other event can equal. Montague is full of strange mystical stories — Verandah finding a letter in her attic from Marshall — she knows when it would have been written and sent but ~~never~~ can't remember reading it before — that reads like a letter from beyond the grave — it was just lying there in an envelope with her name on it. Jon Maslow gave John Wilton three stories just before Jon Marshall's totally unexpected death — John didn't read them till after — one turned out to be "An Inquiry into the Suicide of the Fox" — with all the farm people as animals, the fox being Marshall. When M + friends first arrived at the farm, they found a dead fox, his neck inexplicably caught in the forked branch of a tree — do foxes climb trees? Could he have fallen? No one asks.

Things are going down and up. Montague is on the city-energy circuit: 3½ hrs from NY, 2 hrs from Boston — people come and go — the men are restless, the women distant — an outlaw retreat. And a cradle of the new world, almost in spite of itself. Death occurs; but life will triumph. Everyone knows this. But no one knows how.

Marshall (who with Raymond founded Liberation News Service - they have been friends for years) was - I am told by his survivors - a repressed homosexual. Always afraid of admitting it ("it=?") even to himself, Raymond talked to me about this in Donald's house in Mendocino. He said he'd always sort of known that Marshall wanted to make love to him — but Marshall never said so, never asked, the subject never came up. Now Marshall is dead, and Raymond is thinking about it.

What can any of us do but love (and live) all we can in the moment?

And who among us even does that?
As lovers we are all under-achievers.

✕

What the fuck is a "homosexual=? Some sort of an outlaw, by definition fucked-up, a person whose sexual energies are "mis-directed." All my life I have been terrified, perhaps more than anything else, of being "queer." My mother hates queers. For a long time she thought anyone with a beard was queer. She also hates Germans. During the war, she worked at Los Alamos on the Bomb.

That's where she met my father. My
father had never fucked anyone when he married
my mother. Then, around the time my youngest
brother was born, he met someone else
and fucked her.

And married her. After he and my mother
fought it out for six years.

When he left, he told my mother we
would all (three boys) grow up to be queers.

That got to her.

Raymond is a world-saviour. He doesn't
want to be – no one wants to be – Mel didn't
want to be, it terrified him. A world-saviour
is a person who declares his true identity, who
ups the ante of what it is to be a person,
what our collective reality is, regardless of
the cost.

The cost is always an incredibly
heightened vulnerability. Every advance means
a loss of security. The world-saviour cuts
the gordian knot of his own security; He
tries to lift us by our bootstraps. He bares
his neck to the world.

Here is what Raymond wrote in the latest "Occasional Drop":

[Do You Think It Would Hurt Our Relationship If I Asked You to Suck Me Off?]

Well we all know the tangle of pride and dismay which can accompany natural energies of the penis and clitoris. These foolish portions of the anatomy do dictate our lives more than any other. The path of true love never did run smooth, and if we span the globe, pine away, or even slit our throats for love, how can we be held responsible for it? We all have a point to prove in this regard, it seems.

The precise counterpart of our sexual bravado is our sexual shame. Some of us take the shame to our graves, leaving the good to waste. Be not ashamed, dear ones. If you want to make love to me, however you dig it, know that you need only ask, I will never refuse. Do not yourself refuse when someone comes to you. You may not have another chance.

—x

"There will always be a place for you in my
parking lot,... ~

Oh Tom, there's so much happening in
our lives. On our trip, I bared my neck to you
and you didn't strangle me. Do you remember
that? And you revealed your desire to me,
and I did not respond.
    What is the difference between desire and
need? I don't know, I do not know.
    But there was so much happening. I had
raved my world-saviour rant and you and Lark
and Judy had disappeared.
    And gotten together. That made me very
happy. It still does. It is right.
    We should be together...
    I couldn't make love to you on that
acid-trip.
    For one thing, I don't know what it means.
When I love a woman, I touch her—perhaps her
face, gentle hand on a cheek; she touches me, perhaps

Just a hand on mine, encouragement, affirmation of what's happening. We continue to caress and touch in natural progression and know beyond doubt the growing affection and love in each contact which must try harder and harder to come out, express itself, driving us closer and closer to each other's genitals, the first touch to her crotch, first reach for my hard cock incredibly exciting, the beginning of the home stretch, coming together, that feeling which is so much for that other person soon pulls me into her and her around me, it is unavoidable, inevitable, unbelievable, it unfolds naturally from that first touch.

Can that happen between you and me? I don't know. I have never desired a man in the sense that I constantly desire various women, and this makes sense to me because men don't have cunts that I could come into, which is what my woman-desire ultimately is or how it expresses itself.

I don't want to come into your cunt, Tom, it is too clear to me that you don't have one. But I do want to touch you. And I love you.

what are we going to do about it?

what are we going to do about it?

Charles Manson essay

    Listen, this is a difficult piece to write, because I want to make
things clear & what we're dealing with here is Life Magazine reality
assumptions and most of us are in varying stages of outgrowing these &
that makes it hard to make things clear.   The thing is,   there is
a real paucity of things you can feel sure of these days. It's hard
to just float and perceive things around you without a place to stand
of your own. But I suppose that's what we're learning to do.
    Why? Because we're beginning to realize we--people--are not as smart
as we thought & we're in way over our heads & we have to simplify our
world (s) quite a bit before we can again begin to assume things. For
the moment, absolute ambiguity is the only reality. We are moving into
Tower-of-Babel times.
    Which is fine, unless you're somebody who thinks he can't let go.
    Listen to this: (<u>Life</u> on the subject of Manson)
            "He sensed something old as tribal blood ritual which
            most of us deny in ourselves--that humans can feel
            enormous fulfillment and enormous relief in the act of
            killing other humans if some medicine man applauds and
            condones the deed."
Doesn't it sound as though the man who wrote those words and the men who
edited them really had no idea they were talking about the U.S. Army?
Not just My Lai, not just Vietnam, not just the U.S. armed forces in fact
but all military operations everywhere...
            "Charlie was able to attune his time-encrusted con-
            cepts of villainy to the childish yearnings of his
            hippie converts--to their weaknesses, their catchwords,
            their fragmentary sense of religion and their enchant-
            ment with drugs and idleness--and to immerse them in
            his own ego and in idiotic visions of apocalypse."
    The next paragraph starts: "It is hard not to wince..." Imagine a man
who finds it hard not to wince. Okay.
    Now go back up there and change the word "hippie" to "human".
    Change the word "Charlie" to "Adolf" or "Jesus". Stick in your own
name and see what happens.

                              *

    I don't know if any of this stuff <u>Life</u> says about Manson is true,
they sure talk as tho it is (whatever happened to "alleged" assassin and
all that bullshit?), I doubt they could make up such a true-to-life
story (tho parts of it sure are reminiscent of Rudy Wurlitzer's novel <u>Nog</u>),
anyway it doesn't matter, only the princess and the prince discuss what's
real and what is not, the rest of us just wallow in it.
    He certainly sounds disgusting. I find it difficult to tolerate
people who let themselves enjoy being cruel. That includes me when I
catch myself. Manson can claim society has given him a lot of shit (much
of his adult life spent in prison) but society has given all of us a lot
of shit, only corporate liberals accept that kind of excuse (or any kind
of excuse...you can't back out of karma).
    That bit about Manson and <u>Stranger</u> is worth exploring further, even
if that news story I saw was just a hallucination (Carolanne   saw it too).
A lot of us hippies have read <u>Stranger</u> <u>in</u> <u>a</u> <u>Strange</u> <u>Land</u> somewhat more
closely than the <u>Bible</u> (which Manson is also into) or <u>Portnoy's</u> <u>Complaint</u>.

Manson, if he was preaching the gospel according to Saint Heinlein,
was no more attentive than most preachers: "A Martian is never butchered
against his will. In fact, murder doesn't seem to be a Martian concept.
A Martian dies when he decides to..."
                                        Of course, what Manson plucked
out of Stranger (on the subject of death; no doubt he had an excellent
rap on pan-sexuality..no doubt still does. Why do I think of him in the
past?) was probably the bit about "How can he be dead when no one can be
killed?" (says Jill at the end of the book; the earlier quote was Jubal's.
Find 'em yourself.)
                                       part
     Ah, ah. The theme of the third chapter of More Than Human (I think.
I wish I could stop writing long enough to reread all this stuff.) -- when
supermen start emerging, what you gonna do for a transitional morality?
(transition between old culture and new; new being defined by the time
when man as a whole has attained the new consciousness-state   that is
presently coming on in flashes...longer and longer ones).

     Time between: it is awfully hard to realize that death is not to be
feared and still cling to old-morality codes against killing.

     Time between: so stop bridging the gap and start finding your new
morality now. New morality is not based on fear, a wrathful god, it's based
on intuitive awareness of ecology and karma. "If you want to get to heaven/
Over on the other shore/Stay out of the way of the gun-shot devil..."
You are what you eat. So cannibalism is unavoidable. Embrace it. But
if you act hate (cruelty, revenge) you are hate and dig how attractive
that is. Murder and suicide are OUT in my world-system (morality) because
...uh...they are on the side of entropy.
                              We are on the side of life.

We must act accordingly.

                                *

     This is all just   barely clear, but close enough. The emergence of
supermen--world-saviours, if you will; I would include Mel, Sirhan,Leary etc--
is to me just the historical process of the emergence of real men, i.e. persons
living in the present before it's obvious to most people what the present is.
So the emergence of such strong men and myths (Stranger, which is also Tommy;
the evolutionary myth as explored by Arthur Clarke in Childhood's End and the
flic 2001 is another worth mentioning;   likewise the parapsychic gestalt
of More than Human and the nature-loving survival-oriented invincible clansmen
of Dune) is a natural part of the emergence, as viewed from here, of the new
order (out of the present chaos), the Aquarian Age, Wayne McGuire's myth of
the World Brain and the Sacred Heart of Christ. Life Magazine: "Charlie
preached a confused but vehement philosophy. Everything in the world belonged
to all its people--thus   there could be redivision of valuables, but no
theft; all humans were part of some homogenous and mystic whole--thus there
could be no   real death." I'll buy that, if you'll just let me throw in
Eliot Rosewater:
          Goddamn it, you've got to be kind

Maybe Life Magazine would dig a slightly less confused philosophy;
here's William Buckley, from his syndicated column, on the value of
human life:

> "The   enemy in Vietnam retains the technical
> capacity to regenerate himself at about the
> rate at which we have been killing him. An es-
> timated 100,000 healthy males not designated
> for specialized training turn 18 every year.
> That is about how many soldiers on an average
> have been killed per year over the course of the war.
> " The bright side of   it, in the macabre
> figuring of the military statisticians, is that
> something like an entire generation of North
> Vietnamese males has been killed during the past
> seven years. The sobering side is that they grow
> 'em as fast as we kill 'em."

As for Manson's hypnotic powers, well maybe. But   haven't powerful
personalities always attracted followers, supporters of one sort or
another? Maybe Manson's family reminds you   of the family in the
nest in Stranger. But doesn't it also remind you of the Kennedy boiler
room girls?

> (my theory, by the way, is that
> she was driving the car. Or didn't
> you see Jules and Jim?)

The strong survive.

Manson controlled people through fear and strength, repetition and
reason. The   very techniques employed by western society, the U.S. government, American corporations. But the techniques don't matter (though
"fear" is a key word); the very fact of control, need for control, desire
for control is degenerate, inorganic, immoral, an anachronism in the
Aquarian Age.

> (Fear of control is also bullshit, tho I still suffer from it.
>   No one can control you; you and the universe are the only powers
>   that exist. Take   command of   your own life; don't let
>   nobody tell you what to do, but when you see truth embrace it.
>   Don't be intimidated. That's an order.)

Charlie Manson kind of low in consciousness in a lot of ways, but
still higher than most of   us, he believes in himself and his own perception of the world and that's step number one. Know yourself; affirm
your identity. That's the beginning. Then you can start up the road of a-
wareness. Charlie hasn't gotten too far, says me; but I'm going to have
to be stronger than him if I'm going to make that statement stick, if my
higher view is to prevail (and be transcended). Stronger than Manson?
That's some challenge; I guess I've got my work cut out for me. These
world-saviours keep pulling me upward.

> ~~The strong survive.~~ We can all survive, if we choose to.

I would like to announce, in case there are some who are not
aware of it, the complete and final collapse of the moral basis
of western civilization, the Old World.
    (yes the very same Old World whose churches, schools, jails,
    franchise restaurants, courthouses and gas stations dot the
    landscape)
        (yes the very same moral code that underlies the
    righteousness of all parents and parent figures ("grown-ups")
    (Al Capp, Hayakawa, Richard Nixon, J. Edgar, the Pope) every-
    where)
        (yes the very same...)

I have been reading a "Talk of the Town" essay in The New Yorker
on the subject of the massacre at My Lai, Quang Ngai Province,
South Vietnam. It is a very reasonable essay.

It in no way suggests that there is anything any of us can do
to retain our self-respect.   I was going to quote the essay here,
but it is too dismal, the collapse of the Old World is not a part
of my story here except insofar as you must accept that collapse
as fact, as final, before you can begin to struggle with the dif-
dicult, ambiguous, frightening, joyous realities I perceive.

The essay is too reasonable. No one can outreasonable Talk-of-the-
Town writers, no one is better skilled at performing
            the myth of the moderate man.
    So I think it only reasonable to request that we
                   bury the myth

dig no holes in the ground

you cannot hide; you need not hide

this is revolution; we can all take part; it is a process of
          shedding the skin

       molting

so let's not fool around any more, there is nothing, nothing, no
part of the superstructure worth clinging to, preserving
    there are only shards, and the shards will stay with us
    the noble works of man, his courage, his genius
       but no trace of the old skin,
          let us no longer carry that around

it is time to stand naked, vulnerable virgin hide
beneath the sun
no security, no protection but no death-mask to keep out the life-giving
    forces   we can survive

who clings to his old skin will perish

no blame

But I'm addressing this to you my reader who has gotten this far
        accepted this much intimacy
I assume you do not want to perish
        assume you even know that you need not perish
            assume you are not a creature
                    who is blind to the inevitable

so let us shed our skins now

do not go to school in the morning

do not go to work in the morning

not if you have any doubts, <u>any</u> doubts
        about the massacre at My Lai
        or the way that we treat this planet
        or the honesty of your love relationships

 not if you have any doubts, <u>any</u> doubts
        about where you fit in to all this

did you create the school?
        is it work that your heart embraces?
    did you create the day?

our purpose here is to create the day

we must not spend energy in service to old ideas
            we must not be the props supporting the skeleton
                of a world & world-concepts whose very flesh
                have been eaten away by time

so I ask you very specifically,
                why are you going to college?
        did you create the college?
            you support the college
        all students support the system
        all citizens support the state

did you spend money on oil today?
    do you dream of dead pelicans?
        do you dream of dead planets?

do not go to world today

not that world   today's the day   declare a new world
        live a new world
        it is up to we

            burn your possessions
                abandon all certainty
            use your skills

anyone who reads this and goes to school in the morning is a fool

I am here to announce the collapse of the old moral code
            and that means everything

        whatever seeds you have that won't grow when you put them in earth
    forget them
        they are worthless

        whatever abilities you have that won't help you survive
        unless things stay the way they are
            abandon them
        they are obviously worthless

    ooh, well the storm is threatening
            are you working for dollars
            at a mill somewhere
            when hammer and axe alone
            can give you shelter

                    are you singing for pennies?
                    are you some kind of fool?

can't buy you love   ooh yes, you're gonna fade away

        I told Frank Herbert that the man who wrote Dune would
        never need a dollar again in his life, his energy balance
        is paid up, the people will support him

        and then I went north and Harold who will soon be my
        neighbor asked me if I'd read "Muad'Dib" and I said
        Frank and Beverly were thinking of moving north with us
            and he said, "I'll build him a house!"
        Harold builds good houses.

            I'm not sure you can buy a good house, these days.

there is nothing any of "us" can do to retain our self-respect.
            after Fred Hampton's murder
            after the My Lai massacre
            after younameit

        but goddamn it! Don't you know, after reading this far
    that we're only part of that "us" by choice?
                free your mind instead (easily said)

            well okay, if you don't think you can get free of the Old World
            and its values & comforts & ensnaring convictions
            okay

this is just to let you know that we're leaving you here to rot.

                    ("don't you think there's a place for you...?")

ANYONE WHO'S AFRAID OF ME, GET THE HELL OUT OF HERE
RIGHT NOW!

we should be together

(letter from Carolanne)

Greco--
  God! I have been thinking about you for over a week--
constantly! Everyone I see either looks like you (or Janice,
and I think of you) or reminds me of something common to us
both.
  I'm in New York right now. Paul is on a publishing expedition and I'm following. I've just spent a week in Cambridge
seeing Darcy & Sally & friends of mine & Bird's & Paul's.
  I hate New York. It makes me physically sick. I don't have
the right kind of energy I guess, at least for what we're doing & where we are, and what energies I do have just get frustrated making me miserable all around. I don't understand it
'cause I really like Boston. But New York isn't Boston I
guess. I remember your saying that you liked New York better
than Boston. Maybe it depends hell I don't care.
  (Bear (?) with me I have some poison circulating and I have
to let it out.)
  Anyway it was really good to talk with ol' Darcy again.
She filled me in on most of the latest FPC-related gossip and
between her & Janie--whom I called and Janice--who called
Darcy--I seem to at least be able to keep track of some people.
I've been pretty isolated I guess and haven't been overanxious
to write anyone.
  I guess I should try and contact a lot of people this trip.
Our 'family' is moving to British Columbia in March. Paul & I
& others are moving to a piece of land--180 acres about 150
miles N. of the city of Vancouver--on the coast--beyond the end
of the road (accessible only by boat). There are some people
living there now who own the land who are going to let us build
houses until we decide to move or buy our own land. It's sur-
prisingly really nice! Right on the Georgia Straight (fish &
seafood all year round) warmed by the Japanese Current (it
rains in the winter--no or little snow), mountains to the east,
Vancouver 7 hrs. away to the south and hopefully by winter at
least 50 friends living nearby. There are at least that many
fr. Mendocino, and I am sure Sue will come & George & Michael
fr Boston & on & on...
  I'm going to get a camera tomorrow (or in the next few days)
I told my aunt to fuck off after she pulled a spying job on me
and she decided she wasn't going to get me the camera for grad-
uation so we're going to get one here in N.Y. A different kind
of course... There will be no electricity in B.C. for enlarging
so I will have to make trips to the nearest town (20 mi?) peri-
odically. Am excited but I have gone thru so many hassles w/my
aunt & Paul about it since last Sept. it's a touchy thing.
Don't know.
  Just slept for about 3 hours. Woke up and was very surprised
to discover my throat felt about 2 times normal size and 2 ear
aches. I'm sure it's probably just a reaction to the change in
climate --going from 60° to -14° to 40° again. My body's just
not used to these things. Florida winters have been treating it
good.
  I just ripped up a page I started, containing a whole bullshit rap about love & lovers & friends & acquaintances and after

re-reading the paragraph came to the conclusion that personal
relationships exist in a direct time-space relationship and
trying to say whether someone is a 'lover' or 'someone you love'
is a ridiculous distortion. Nevertheless, true to my inconc-
sistent nature I have discovered that I still love you even
though I haven't seen you for almost a year and we are 3000 miles
apart. So relatioships exist outside of a time-space setting.
Fuck. And I was always your fantasy-lover--does it matter?
No, it doesn't. I love you still, that's all that matters for
that's all I know. Self doubt: am I going to be misinterpreted
again in my love? Does my love of Paul & Michael & Carl mean or
change anything about my love for you in your mind. It does I
guess. I don't know. You don't have to worry tho--I'm not going
to jump on the next plane for St. Petersburg and fall at your
feet crying I love you Rick. /editor's note--that last sentence
was crossed out in the original./ I'm getting tired and confused
that last sentence was stupid & incoherent. Forgive me--I'll write
again tomorrow.

A new day, a new year. The year 1 of course. From now on it's
always the year one. Last year was -1, right now next year is 2,
but when next year comes it'll be year one again. Always the year
one, always a new day in a new year. A nice fresh start.
It was hot last night. I don't know what the temperature of the
room was but even a sheet wasn't needed. I'm not used to that and
it was uncomfortable. I like to snuggle in blankets.
Off to work, so to speak. To E.P.Dutton for more hassling about
Paul's next book, jacket designers, copy editors Paul's editor &
the managing editor, a whole hierarchy of middlemen, useless, time
consuming and confusing. The perfect publisher: one who would take
your book and print it? A dream? Made possible, yet aesthetically
not as pleasing to middle-class book-buying America, by the xerox.
IBM composers run by friends? --Monetary limitations. Next book
will be at camera-copy stage to begin with. Have you read Informed
Sources? The death of Robin the cock? Only now as I wrote it down
did I connect with cock robin? It's not a gross book but it's an
obscene book. Obscene news reports and senseless messages. Distinc-
tion: the book itself is not obscene, the material it covers is.
Another book (damn subway) Van Gogh self portrait. A horrible book
if you're not inside of Van Gogh. Very mellow if you are. Do you
remember the museum in Boston? Of course you do. Well there was
one picture by Van G (a man just sat on my book as I was writing)
that I spent maybe 3 hours looking at. It was called The Ravine.
I tried to get a copy or even a postcard of it but as usual my
choice of masterpieces did not coincide with art critics' choices.
It was (is) fantastic. It was done in the style, the frenetic whirl-
ing chaotic swirls of brilliant colors characteristic of his paint-
ings done in a psychotic state of mind. It was then, looking at
that picture, when I first realized I think, that I was psychotic
too. I didn't know it in those terms--of being psychotic--but I
think I do now. It is said psychotics don't know that they are
psychotic which is why I'm pretty sure that I am--because I don't
know it either. The time will come I think when psychotics will
win out and will control the world--or do they or are they beginning to already? Neurotics will not be able to stand the world long
enough to survive and will die out or kill themselves off. A new

race, the next evolutionary jump must be to a breed of psychotics which will then become the norm for the existing universe. (Damn revolutionary subway car refuses to run. We have been sitting here for 10 minutes now trying to go. Ah! The old way wins out--the 14th St local rolls on... I guess it was just waiting...   Timing is important, you know. I'm just beginning to realize that timing is another disguise of Fortuna Fate or whatever you want to call it, and that it really conditions our lives.

Somwhere there's a piece written by Carl Jung about astrology, the I Ching and the Tarot. I haven't read the article, but this guy was rapping to me about how Jung valued the I Ching and the Tarot as an outlet for the functioning of the personal unconscious against the collective unconscious. The I Ching contains the collective unconscious of the universe and when we throw a hexagram we are pulling to the conscious level, through chance, a segment of it for consideration. Astrology, however, only allows a finite amount of information to circulate, for example, I have my Mercury in Leo which means blah blah blah...therefore I should act blah blah. No allowance for time,space, energy, anything. Definite rules which are or are not followed

"And every person is a new time."
                    --John Sebastian

Just saw him at the Bitter End--really really good. We were socializing with the president of Elektra Records and he bopped in & told the owner to save a table & we'd be back after dinner. Met John briefly, real nice guy, I guess.

Bought a Pentax yesterday. Anxious to get started. After 5 months of hassle I don't even believe I have my own camera. I gte nervous handling it. Want to get out and shoot some of New York today. Darcy has access to a dark room in Waltham. When I return we were going to try & develop & print up some film but now if she's working...

I guess sickness rightly doesn't mean anything to those who are well and it is good yet hard psychologically that the sick are scorned by the fit. Scorn surfaces things for me. If I feel scorn from someone (Ah yes Sue you were the best at scorning me) it's an immediate blow to my ego, the motion of its falling which I detect. I used to detect it and repress it, only to find it rearing its head in my work in many disguises. Mostly negative forms although I do remember a time or two when I think scorning caused me to change my "erring" ways. One thing I've found, I _have_ to know what's going on in my head-- bad or good. Of course the bad makes me feel worse and I tend to dwell on it, sending myself spiraling down, but I _have to_ _know_ it's there. I have to keep feeling. It seems to me that Paul goes right from the action to its solution without feeling anything or much in between. That's good for him I guess he functions well, when he has his own way (don't be bitter Currier!) Maybe _that_'s the next evolutionary jump--people who instinctively _or_ telepathically do what's right next without waiting for any feedback from previous actions. Maybe that's called self-confidence maybe it's called ego --whatever it's called I don't have it. Maybe I'm a romantic--a sadistic masochistic emotionalist who likes to feel bad as well as good. I can rationalize by saying "you never know when you're up unless you're down" blah blah blah. But either that rationalization isn"t true or I have a really good memory of downs to sustain me through the long periods of highs. However I might suspect the truth lies in the basic fact accepted by my psyche that bad times are just as real as the good time and therefore should be given just as much attention. Obviously everyone (not everyone but certainly some people including Paul) consider this to be a real drag. And consequently knowing that some people consider being down a "real drag" (and my subconscious--and conscious--desire not to bring anyone down that doesn't want to be down--which can be done to some people, not others) I feel worse.

But that's O.K. I really feel that everything's O.K. but sometimes my wires get crossed and a negative charge tries to connect with a positive line, if only positive energy would run down one side of the line and negative up the other the old system would flow pretty smoothly, but judging from the condition of the telephone system here in New York all systems can fuck up pretty bad.

Maybe I'm not a sadistic romantic. Virgoans are not noted for romantic tendencies. Maybe I really don't believe in the existence of bad times, conflicts etc. Maybe I'm so idealistic that I believe everything should be great all the time. And then when they're not, illusions shatter and my dream world falls apart.

Oh well, at least I'm having fun with my camera. It needed a new battery (brand new and it needed a new battery!! Probably had been sitting on the shelf for 2 years (the normal lifetime of a battery)). Took some pictures of David Henderson & Barbara two spade writer friends of Paul's. I still feel shy about taking pictures of people. There was this groovy Sgt-Pepper-looking man on the street the other day and I really wanted a picture of him but he looked at me real strange as if I were, which to him I must have been, so I didn't shoot him. The people who offered to have me take their pictures were a spade bum in the Union Sq park and a fat Jewish businessman: oh-yes-I-have-a-camera-and-isn't-it-great-to-take-pictures-of-friends-and-send-them-to-people-I-have-the-newest-Polaroid! It is fun to send pictures to friends, and the Polaroid is fine for "snapshots," "my vacation" but the trouble with the automatic Polaroid is that it takes a picture of what is being received by the camera's mind not by the cameraman's mind. This might be a challenging limitation to some photographer. However manual,physical, creative processes are denied --and I want all the help I can get!

Hmm... This last paragraph seemed to be a lot of unnecessary bullshit. Who am I trying to convince about what? You know more about cameras and their limitations than I ever will. I almost bought a Minolta by the way, the only reason (differences) I could see for having the Pentax is that it was a little lighter

weight--and for the same price... The Minolta does have the
flip-up mirror do-jiggy which I didn't understand really but
decided it was nothing vital. Oh, I did like the Pentax's screw-
in-lens mount rather than the catch type but then again--when
am I going to be able to afford a telescopic lens? Not soon,
that's for sure. I hope Sue comes back to California when we go
see her and not next summer. (There is a connection between
those last 2 sentences but it's not worth explaining.)

     I threw the coins for the general conditions surrounding
the immediate future and got the same things that I got before
leaving Mendocino. My mind connected with the fact that the
hexagrams were the same and went no further. I don't even really
remember what the text said. I guess I really didn't want to
know. I kind of feel guilty about disobeying my interpretations
of a hexagram I threw in San Francisco. I was trying for a week
to decide whether to go on to Boston with Paul or to stay in
S.F. for a while and then go back home to Mendocino. I got the
hexagram Return. The text is/was in my case ambiguous. I emotion-
ally interpreted it as telling me something hairy would happen
to me if I went. But rationally, literally, I read that things
would be all right if I went, so I did. I feel as though I didn't
follow my intuitive senses in that choice, which I don't like
to do. I'm usually much happier if I follow my intuition and for
quite a while now I have been letting my 'heart' rule and my 'head'
guide. It was the opposite in this case and I hope I won't be
sorry. I can do anything though, I know it!! Negative positive
I can't I can. I freaked out in Cambridge & ended up having Darcy
drive me to the C-bridge hospital on her birthday! Maybe that
was the 'something hairy.' Maybe it's I have to take tranqs to
survive in the city. Maybe it's the city showdown--the parting of
veils--the revealing of the truth of all truths:

                    THE CITY SUCKS!

And city dwellers really are suckers, "trading hits" with their
vacuum cleaning buying and selling racketeers, who, not being
able to slip under the rug soon enough, get swallowed by their
own machines and end up with the rest of the dirt until somebody
will come along and let the dirt out of the bag.

          I'm almost through (I'm Paul again) rereading <u>Stranger</u>

--If I remember right (I'm not rereading <u>TB</u> yet) most of my rap
on Stranger so far has been about the author/protagonist interaction, my ideas about certain kinds of books writing themselves.
No, not writing themselves--it's an exact parallel with my ideas
about life: yin/yang: receptive/creative: I am in control of my
life, my world, but only exactly so far as the world, the universe
is master of me. An author determines what happens in his book;
but if he's a really good author, there is inevitably a balance
between what he causes and what he allows to happen, receptive,
a given situation, place time & characters, must develop in a
certain way no matter what the author wants, if you try to stand
in the way of the natural flow of things you don't end up with
a plot but a hemmorhage.
          I know some of you understand this point
of view <u>and</u> the language I'm using; but some probably don't, and
it's important, so I'll try to elucidate:
                                        At any given moment
in my life, there are decisions to make if I think there are
(which is less and less often, these days). At the simplest level,
the decision is usually whether or not to act--whether to let
things happen the way they seem to be happening or to make a
conscious effort to cause things to happen a particular way.
Causative--willful--action isn't necessarily in opposition to
the dynamic of the moment; it can be in harmony with it, a boost
of energy; or, very often, there may be no dynamic perceivable to
me, from my point of view nothing's happening. Usually if nothing's
happening and I feel something wants to happen I act willfully, I
do something about it. If something's happening and I perceive it,
more often than not I let it happen, I mean since it wants to
happen it's probably right, it's god's will unless it obviously
isn't, unless it feels wrong. The effort is to, well, <u>grok</u> what it
is that's happening, why it wants to happen, how it relates to me,
how it fits in with the cosmic purpose or my plans for the next
few hours or whatever.
                      This may seem complicated, but it isn't; just
remember I'm not theorizing here, I'm just reporting--not trying
to tell you how to think, just telling you what happens (to me--
what else do I know about?).
                           So sometimes I act, do bring about
what I need or what needs to happen (which includes preventing a
wrongness), & sometimes I act but receptively, I let things happen,
because after some thought I can dig the flow (or it just feels good)
and I don't want to stop it up, I want to encourage it. And most
of my actions are neither completely seizing the day nor letting
go to the inevitable, but a little of each
                                          and by now you can dig
that consciously or unconsciously I'm trying to create the I Ching here
from scratch--which isn't so strange; when I was a math student I
more than once invented calculus to solve a trig problem (like the
area under a curve on a graph) & all of us have invented multipli-
cation (when it was too much effort to add)--I'm just looking at
what I know about my life and the way things happen, and I'm saying
that there are purely creative moments and purely receptive ones,
and then there are easily 62 other kinds of situations in which
some lines are receptive and some creative, some male some female,
and if you want to be able to deal with the dynamic you've got to
have a feeling for the energy pattern.   (How about a Broadway
show in which 6 boys & 6 girls act out the hexagrams?)

Decisions to make if I think there are. How often does an
author decide what's going to happen in his book?
                        Not very often, if it's going well.
            So who's in control? The author?
                        Yes, but also the book, that is, the universe
        which is anything (everything) but the author, and can be
        personified in the protagonist, central character, unifying
        force in the novel. The created. Who is himself creator, and inevitably
                changes the author's life.

My rap about my life is that half of it I cause, the other half
happens to me. No half here and half over there, but intertwined,
a delicate shading, all textures from light to dark,
                                        pole to pole.
                Dynamic.

My rap about Stranger is that Heinlein doesn't invent a plot but
plants it, lets it grow--and so comes up with something very real,
realer than he or any of us could have imagined.
                                        Because what will
grow in really fertile, self confident (willful) and utterly receptive soil   is the spirit of the times, the heart of unconscious
man,   the hexagram of the moment
                myth-description of NOW in the life of this being
        and this being is life on this planet.
                        Stranger isn't the daily news
        but it sure is the news, for people who want to deal
        with this moment in history, this period of three-dozen
        years or god knows how many
                                Stranger and not too many other
        works of art will tell you what's happening.
            Another good method is talking to trees.

Is Heinlein (as Stranger-author) the helpless tool of the spirit
of man, the collective unconscious?
Hell no, he's just a man
                        consulting the oracle.
            His reading is 414 pages long & available from
                                Berkley Books.
If you haven't read it in the last six months, prepare to have
                        your mind blown.

        You can reread a given hexagram many times y'know
    By the time there's nothing more to be learned from it, you'll
no longer need the I Ching.

        And you'll probably be a world-saviour.

Meanwhile you really should be working, whatever way seems right
to you, to get there.

        We need your help you know.

(I guess you know   you can write this book
yourself   & believe me I'll be glad to read it
        or meet you when you've finished
                    'cause by that time we may be ready to help each other
            with some other stuff)

(when I say I want to make love to you I guess I also mean
        I want to save the world with you
      which is probably the same
                Vonnegut wasn't ready to say it in 1962 but
            here's what Bokononists say when they (drop acid) make love
            "Now I create the whole world.")

(Don't bother coming to see me if you're in any way afraid of me
        or not ready to give as much as you get
                    or vice versa
        but if you're ready and that's what you want,
        feel free to write or visit
            PW, Refuge Cove, British Columbia
                or maybe I'll visit you

    if you're ready, if you think you're doing right
        and getting a little better at it every day
      which means working harder, don't kid yourself
            but working harder is easier than not, that's the nice part
      you probably shouldn't come till you've at least
            written your own oracle
    in water, earth, air or fire
        In B.C. we have no time for incompetence
                            incompetents?
        Are you a good fuck?
            (why would anyone answer that "no"?
                you are a good lay if you think you are.
                    don't lie to yourself))

(Am I ready?   Brother, I don't know.
        But I'm going to B.C. in March to build my house,
            and I'll let you know what happens next.)

            now I create the whole world...

P.S: Anybody visiting us in Galley Bay, house gifts are appreciated. Organic whole grains, fresh & dried fruit, ~~cassettes of~~
music you really love, books ditto, yarn, material, prints by
Monet or Van Gogh, fine wines, anything you grew or made yourself. No garbage. Uh, organic peanuts, brandy & spear-heads for
Alan. Organic tobacco for Carl & Harold. Nails. Mantles for the
Aladdin lamps. Don't expect to sleep indoors if you come in
the summer. Don't expect to stay very long very close to where
anyone else has his life to live. Sleeping bag and tent for
yourself, therefore. You can't get to us by car: prepare to
swim or bribe a fisherman. Don't come to hang around; this ain't
a summer resort, it's a planet.

Visitors are a problem at every commune, every new-style home
I know of. They're a problem because as a rule they function
at lower energy than everyone else. So they drag you down, cause
friction. I intend to see to it that we don't have any visitors.
Just members of the family.

You're welcome anywhere, any time, if you bring energy to exchange,
interact with the energy that attracted you. The only way for me
to let everyone know or begin to learn they're welcome anywhere
is to tell you you're welcome where I am. You are. But don't think
I'm here to help you. I'm here to help us. You better be too.

If you're not, you're part of a dying race.

/quotes from Stranger--think of this first one as Michael Heinlein
 speaking to Jubal Heinlein:7

"   /MH7 'It was what I started out to do. It is not what
I am trying to do now. Father, I know that you were disappointed
in me when I started this.'
     /JH7 'Your business, son.'
          'Yes. Self. I must grok each cusp alone. And so must
you ... and so must each self. Thou art God.'
          'I don't accept the nomination.'
          'You can't refuse it. Thou art God and I am God and
all that groks is God, and I am all that I have ever been or
seen or felt or experienced. I am all that I grok. I saw the
horrible shape that this planet is in and I grokked, though not
in fullness, that I could change it. What I had to teach couldn't
be taught in schools...'   "

/Michael on blowing up Earth by willpower:7
     " 'I have the discipline to do it,.. but not the volition.
The essence of the discipline is, first, self-awareness, and
then, self control. By the time a human is able to destroy this
planet by this method--instead of by clumsy things like cobalt
bombs--it is not possible, I grok fully, for him to entertain
the volition. He would discorporate.' "

"   /Duke:7 'Jubal, there's something about Mike that makes you
want to take care of him.'
          'I know. You've probably never encountered honesty
before. Innocence. Mike has never tasted the fruit of the Tree
of Knowledge of Good and Evil ... so we don't understand what
makes him tick.' "

          ("We are stardust, we are golden
           And we have got to get ourselves back to the Garden."
                         --Joni Mitchell, via CSN&Y)

"   /Jubal:7 'Whenever anyone comes here to live, I make it
plain that this is neither a sweat shop nor a whore house, but
a home ... and, as such, it combines anarchy and tyranny without a trace of democracy, as in any well-run family, i.e., they
are on their own except where I give orders, which orders are
not subject to debate.'   "

"   /Mike:7 '"Thou art God." It's not a message of cheer and hope,
Jubal. It's a defiance--and an unafraid unabashed assumption of
personal responsibility.' "

"   /Jubal:7 'If one tenth of one percent of the population is
capable of getting the news, then all you have to do is show
them--and in a matter of some generations the stupid ones will
die out and those with your discipline will inherit the Earth.' "

just called home--it's Feb 3, Aquarius something, year one--
     here's the news:
               Tom & Judy in the city for the last 3 days,
                    some kind of separation between Lark & them
                Lark doesn't understand what but it's okay
                not upset now; we all come together in time
               Tami freaked a while back, much screaming
               Tom sat on her & wouldn't let her leave till
               everything was resolved & everyone tried to
               help her and talk with her but...
               she's in the city now, probably at Margaret's
                    or Tung's
                    Alan got a very nice letter from her today
               Alan's been with Lark
                    Lark says: in my darkest hour, there he was
                    she's very happy Alan really comes thru in a pinch
                    I'll bet he's happy too
                    he was asleep when I called, so the full Alan
                    report will have to wait
                    but they've been making very good love
               the dogs are fine
               Thistle very happy, thinking of going to Hong Kong
                    but thinking of BC too, I really want her to
                    go up with us--know she will sooner or later but
                    sooner would be nice
                    Yarrow's happy all the time
                    Thistle says when she's down she   just picks up
                     on Yarrow's good vibes
                    she got a letter from Donald
                    in Vera Cruz--nice letter
                    Thistle wishes he wouldn't have written her a
                    nice letter--she wants to be free of him
               It was so good talking to her & Lark
               being in touch with the family
                    god I feel good about all of them, close to them
                    I just finished reading Stranger &
                    I feel the warmness of family & absence of distance
                    separation it's really high
               Andy's sick, Lark too, Robinson told her to
                    make love a lot, what a fine doctor
               Andy & Judy, Ron & Kay there but no news
               Michael & Kathy gone north, Carolanne misses them
                    but we'll meet again
               Playboy sent the check for $178, I told them
                    Wdstock expenses were $578 and they believed me
                    or didn't care if it was true or not ($400 advance)
               Thistle may go to Oklahoma, Alan wants to go to
                    Mexico but is waiting for me to come home, or
                     Donald--I wish I were going to be home sooner
                    than three weeks but I can't help it, I'm caught
                    by this publishing thing--hope he just goes to
                    Mexico whenever it feels right, don't wait for us
                    (guess he thinks there shd be a man in the hse)
There may have been more news but that's what I remember,
          the important thing is everything's fine, most are
          happy &
          going thru changes

want to write more but tired of this typewriter.....
tomorrow to Raymond's — see you all there!

ONE !!!

Vot ya ee Raymond's
 That's Russian, and it means: here I am at Raymond's
place in Vermont, it's four below zero and there aren't
any periods on this typewriter, so if I feel like
stopping I'll use a slash/

I'm still Paul, I feel a need to say that because
I don't know if I will be much longer, it's never
been entirely clear to me who was writing this book,
I mean I know it's me but I don't know who else it is or I am
yeah I know I don't grok in fullness who I am, and
every day and every book
 I find out a little bit more

not to mention the constant skin-shedding/I'm younger than that now

 Let's call this page one of Time Between, comes
right after page 131 if I remember right/

some people think this book is going back home but
you know you never get there
you have to make it home right where you are

                    I feel good here

high like on the edge of an acid trip, swallowed already and
          nervous tense about to spin off into space
               excited   apprehensive
     (Tension Dissension Apprehension Have Begun
       no, I'm not the Demolished Man
                 this is no world I never made)

          I want to fuck Dale, dance with Raymond,
                    Michael & Carolanne
               (god, the names recur, maybe there are really only
                    as many people as there are names
                         if that--don't try to sort out ambiguity
                    wallow in it)

     on the edge, apprehensive, of some great leap thru time
               back to where I came from and on to where we're going

          oh no, I've no doubts
     I sometimes wonder how I'm doing
     but only in those dull moments when I think I'm doing Something
          it's much more than that

     break on thru!

TWO

Sometimes what is called for is revolution.
My friends here keep telling me things aren't
as "advanced" here as on the west coast.

I don't believe it.
   Things are whatever you want them to be,
   If you have the strength,
   If the time is right.
The way to find out what time it is
   is to speak your mind
   and see what happens.

You can't get burned being honest in public,
   You can only lose "friends" who aren't with
You all the way.

People who aren't with you all the way
are no fucking good at your side in
   times like these.

On your own day you are believed.

The question is:
→ are things "advanced" enough for you?
   (If you try some time, you just might find...)

Something wants to happen?
so it seems
Do _I_ want something to happen?
oh yeah, I alwayslike it when things are happening, unless things
        have been happening for quite a while, and I'm exhausted
and actually, as you very well know, not much has HAPPENED for a
        while now, not since all that stuff with Tom andLark and Judy
        and Carol and Alan and Carl and Michael and so on--
we've just been travelling around & coping with the weather & the publishers
and since nothing's been happening that demanded my full attention
        I've been in my head, talking about Manson and Stranger and
        a lot of thought-associations, ideas, creation/destruction of
        concepts, which I enjoy and I hope makes okay reading and anyway
        with any luck it'll all be good background for what now HAPPENS
        but who knows if anything's going to happen,
            gee I sure hope so/

'Course this is Raymond's house & I'm not entirely sure if _he_ wants
        something to happen
Verandah does, but R maybe does & doesn't, y'know, ambivalence
    who are we to tell anyone how to resolve his ambivalence?
 To tell anyone anything you have to assume some stuff that is at
    the very least subject to challenge
So I guess as long as I make it clear enough that I'm always subject to
    challenge, and even often Wrong
    I can speak my mind
 But it isn't really my mind I want to speak, it's the group's mind
Whoever the group is
            and whatever we want to say   to ourself
You know I don't know
                I'm just fishing

        well Carolanne says lots has been happening but
            she guesses I meant sexual stuff
        that caught me by surprise
        I just meant the kind of stuff that's immediate enough for
    me to write down, like the early pages of this book, I
    don't think I've made conscious decisions about what that stuff
    is, I just write what I can when I can
    but maybe a lot of that stuff is "sexual"
            I wonder what that means?

Hypothesis: I dunno what "sexual" is but it's some kind of energy
    maybe (seems reasonable) it's the same kind of energy that's high enough
(or something enough) to be real on the page, maybe "immeidiacy" is a key word
and when the sexual flow is fast and free the interchange on all levels is
                                        likewise
    or maybe that kind of high energy, caused merely by event-configuration,
        so turns us on & frees our souls that a lot of good sex goes with it
        coincidentally as it were

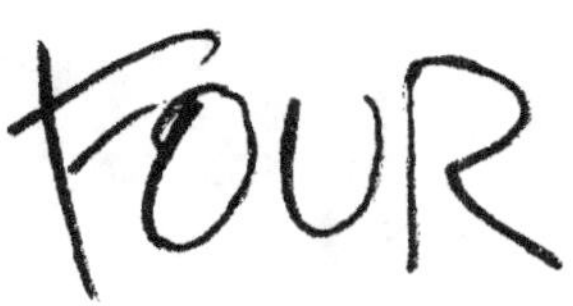

the flow of energy is always what's happening
     and so many factors affect it
 for any individual there's that creative/receptive relationship with it
 but also there's realizing how different each moment is
              so be careful about assumptions
              and trust your intuition
                 and which is which it's subtle
        but not really difficult

Carolanne wrote this last night & brought it in cause of what I
     just read her of the previous page (confluence--well of course,
               we're in the same energy flow,
          shouldn't we notice many of the same things?):

          I'm wary of making any judgments about
          how I feel here yet/ I realize what a span
          of emotions I went through at Jesse's in
          3 (?) days/ Also I'm beginning to associate
          some of the feelings with things like: Just
          walking in after having been travelling (mo-
          tion), how many people you're involved with
          (are you the center of attention, etc), how
          much I already know about the situation I'm
          walking into/ I know now I feel good with
          Raymond here/ I actually feel rather close
          to him/ Paul wrote a page tonight for his
          book and one of the things he mentioned was
          he wanted to fuck this girl here, and mentioned
          me with another fellow named Michael (we're
          once again searching for a change in fucking
          patterns) but if there were anyone here I would
          want to make love to it would be Raymond/ But
          it would be in a veryloving, close, friendly
          way/ I don't feel any special sexual attraction
          to him, I don't even imagine he's a very good 'lay'
          but I would want to make love with him anyway/
          (He just walked in and I jumped/ He's going to
          see if he can find me some long underwear/)

Now of course printing this stuff, I mean typing it here where other people
living here are going to read it, probably   today, is a funny thing, it
makes us all slef-conscious and also kind of forces us to deal with some
stuff we knew is true but--- the Heisenberg uncertainty bit really applies
here, you change a situation by the act of observing it, so there is no such
thing as an "outside" observation, well here we're using the act of observation almost consciously to affect the situation, not in a particular way, no
one can know or even really guess what's going to happen but it seems likely
that if we start telling each other the truth and also listen to each other,
which when a thing's written down you sort of have to do , something's going
to HAPPEN   that is, given the assumption that we're not telling each other
 everything or enough for now already

                                        it's weird---

FIVE

GMP out on the stands!
Almost all of PC reads the GMP!

Oops, I'm slipping into another dimension
Hello, John/ Haven't we been here before?
oh yeah & I now remember
how much I loved it the last time through

Soon after Avatar NY 7 Don died
LNS/LNS split
me to the country, Marshall to the country
Raymond already there
John left the country (I now remember) (Marrakesh?)
later returned to pay it back
Wayne back to Boston & nearer to Mel
scattered
together?
well maybe still

or again, or for the Very First Time, don't you know?

and now Sir John has done the Green Mountain Post
formerly New Babylon Times

descendant and reminder (but it's a whole new world) of NY Avatar
god we really have changed
god, we're really still together

Every joy is another breakthrough/

Raymond rates GMP on a level with Zap Comix and he's right of course
howmany in the audience have heard of Zap Comix?
how many eat breakfast, usually?
Thank you, you may sit down/

I know I'm only talking to my friends/
I don't know how many that is///

Green Mountain Post is a magazine-reader's magazine, every comma is well taken it shifts moods, everything in it is ~~REAL~~ REAL, nothing in it is stupid, fatuous or appalling, it is an expression of HIGH CONSCIOUSNESS, yes i know they say that about everything but this isn't everything it's just a real small real thing & it tickles my head so much i just laugh and sigh

Oooh yes well the storm is threatening
        I feel so confused
 hope it means what it usually means,'cause
      I'd rather break thru than be frustrated

I Ching just told me: Influence to Keeping Still

Raymond wrote the bottom of the last page
 if it makes a difference

John Wilton's Green Mountain Post is certainly the finest publication
        I have read in a long time, not to mention
             my most satisfying public appearance in all of Year One
                  to date

and we dropped by Montague, I believe it was last night,
and got a very good hit from the people there: Johnny, Stevie D,
Stevie M, Evann, Cathy, Tom, Laz, others; it was a quick visit
but invigorating
   I got two letters
        one from John one from Steve M
        both turn-ons/letters help you realize that you're real
                        & friends care

much is in process here (meaning Packer Corners Vt or my head) but
        none of it clear yet
    who knows what shapes will emerge from the swirling mass?
                what swirling mass? you well might ask
        but let's see what the I Ching says:

persistent quiet influence (to stimulate)   joyous response
        attraction between the sexes (Dale? I am endlessly attracted but
                not encouraged, don't know what to do--uncertain, shy)
    ("wooing" is the name of the hexagram too but is there mutual attraction?)
            (and maybe my doubts because I don't know who I am here)
                (which is good if I find out & it's more than who I've been)
Influence Success Perseverance furthers To take a maiden to wife brings good
 fortune
The influence may also refer to my infl on Raymond etc or the farm's infl on me
Hmm, come to think of it I was more asking about what to do or what is happening
   with the book/keeping still within experiencing joy without, are those
   my instructions?
The superior man encourages people to approach him/By his readiness to receive them
        the mind should be kept humble and free
        People soon give up counseling a man who thinks he knows everything better
        than anyone else (yes that sounds like it's aimed at me)

Now the lines (top three)   far out! 9 in 4th Persev brings gd fortune,
 Remorse disappears   If a man is agitated in mind & his thots go hither and
  thither, only those friends on whom he fixes his conscious thots will follow
The commentary tells me to relax and not try to will events at this point, let
influence take its course   okay
In fact, the whole hexagram & its follow-up are trying to tell me to let go
of conscious effort at the moment   also topline warns against tongue wagging
    I can dig it

transition is painful/I trust everything will work out all right

I climbed to the peach orchard   it was much warmer to day   maybe 25°

felt nice   sat in the peach orchard saw the roll of hills
 and valleys   felt like a good place to take acid
 this really is a high place, could see for miles from peach o and all of it fine
sitting on a hill seeing the hills really draws you to the land
            contours

found More Than Human in my pocket in the peach o & started reading
 the third part, called "Morality" in which homo gestalt gets a conscience
 & then merges with the higher consciousness, what men call "God"
 Gerry as a character very reminiscent of Manson
 not just the eyes but bitter tough kid orphanage background
 very high but petty vicious
 leader/spokesman of the gestalt
   as Chester Anderson & David Crosby have noted, the rock group is a
   Sturgeonesque gestalt
   more such will soon emerge, higher forms all the time
    not recognizable as such at first
    but you know what "let's get together" really means
             it means really
        tear down the walls

psychic powers? oh we have 'em   don't kid yourself but we'll probably
 have to get free of primitve technology like jets before we realize

if the family here & our family in Mendocino could get together
        if it could happen
        it would really be something

 like Mel said, it won't be one man this time around in fact, Mel said Christ
said that   Tim Leary also said that to me, tho he was thinking of divine couples
  well Leary's holy couple's a gestalt/ duprass?   I dunno; watch this space

sitting on the snow up the hill in the orchard, reading and looking out
on the Vermont countryside, a peaceful place, a strong place
   not overrun by man, nor wild   healthy

 I still don't wear my glasses and so I don't see detail
   but I could get the feeling of these quiet mountains in the lines I did see
 or somehow perceived and I can still see constellations the stars look different   the textures of the main room, winter room, feel/look fine
    very rich, mellow   people no longer have faces in the familiar sense
 I guess I miss a lot but I see a lot too
           in the gestalt different persons handle different areas of perception
       do your thing

I'm happy here, now that I know my instructions are to keep still & let my
  influence, whatever it is, be felt   I can do that, relax, not feel there's
something I should be doing   write when I feel like it
     gaze on my vague new world   enjoy the weather   smile at friends

eight

this page wants words
there's so much inside of me
how shall I let it out?
who will be left behind?

it's Sunday evening, now, Ray & Carol & Jimmy Jordan
are about to go to Boston
Ray to see movie people flying in from Hollywood
    he wants capital to make a flic/they want his book/his ass
Carolanne to see friends, Darcy & Sally, George whom she
    would like to love, & she has several rolls of film
    to develop
Jimmy along for the ride maybe? Ray maybe back soon if
    he doesn't fly to Montreal (more movie crap) Carolanne
   I'll see on Thursday, when I go in to see Sam Lawrence
 until then, barring the unforeseeable, it's PC for me
I like it here
I'm really beginning to dig the countryside & yes the weather
    maybe because it's been warm for two days, sometimes 50°!
        very nice
Carol and I just went for a walk, the snow and the trees and
    hills and mountains   chasing after the dogs into the woods
    you can't let them go far from you because
        deer feet go thru the crust & dog paws don't
        so the dogs kill many deer
            and the warden'll shoot any dogs he sees
        half a mile into the woods following one dog, calling the
        other two   then back thru the trees up the hill to
        Carolanne   who almost got lost in the woods herself
    and walking back we both knew--it showed on our faces--
    how much we love this place   this land   here

yesterday all day I tried to ped-x an acid trip
            "ped-x" is a Montague word for "peddle"✳
        and Raymond was interested but it never happened
    John interested too but he's got a lot to do
        we went to Montague yesterday, Ray Verandah and I
    Verandah to see an old lover who just blew in from
        a New Jersey Tibetan monastery
    she's surrounded with people she used to live with
            in different places
        all here together all weekend
        Marty, Harry, Jeffrey, Michael
            Ray of course
        the pressure on Verandah was more in her head than in fact
    tho Jeffrey seems to have given her a hard time
            she anticipated that & maybe brought it about
        anyway an interesting situation, it distressed her
            but probably also fascinated
        there won't be more than 8 of us here tomorrow
        maybe less and it's the quieter ones anyway
            should be interesting to see what it's like

I may take acid, all by myself
                or with anyone who wants to
        or go on a long walk, or write a lot
    there's always plenty to do, today we got a bunch of wood
        from the mill, and took out the garbage
        a pick-up truck full
            wood in garbage out   bread & cookies baked
                life on the farm

✳ actually a Packer Corners word that applies to crossing
streets and anything else you have to do that's not high
just to get thoe... from an SF acid trip.

I just built a fire.
We were staying in the main house, where most everyone lives
this time of year in Raymond's room (he slept upstairs)
And then last night Carolanne & I moved out to
        Peter's garden apt.
      above the garage   a small room, all weathered wood
    beautiful very soulful bed in the wall (niche)
        table of a barrel & a slab of wood
            a rocking chair
only the electric light is incongruous   and it's subdued
            I have to check my fire

Carolanne came up & doesn't know if she wants to go now or not
I want her to & that's okay   but how can I say that?
        and she knows... but none of us is ever certain
                of almost anything
        so maybe she doesn't know; and I don't know if I can explain
I want to be alone & more self-indulgent
        for a few days, anyway
      now Carolanne is reading over my shoulder
      "All you have to do is say." "But your feelings might be hurt."
      "Mm hm. They would." "Well, that's no good. Why would they
be hurt?" "Oh, just on general principles."
        Carolanne points out that she didn't mean that last
          statement seriously, which I could tell from her voice
        but maybe you can't tell from her words.
                Anyway, whether something is said "seriously"
        or as a joke, it has the same meaning.
                        But very different impact.
        Everything's okay   I think
            Carolanne pleads the fifth.
        It feels funny to have what you say writ down.
Makes it hard to say anything.

    Bob just came in (he lives in the other part of above-the-garage)
      and said that he & Dale & Michael & Pepper are going to
      Marboro College to see
          The Battle of Algiers
            which I've seen and it had quite an impact on me
        a very important flic   a romantic (?) view of terorism
        but certainly realistic & only propaganda by being sympathetic
    it portrays the horror of the whole thing fully
          and you never know for sure what the "message" is
        but many young people walk out of the theatre eager
                    to become terrorists
          since it's brave work & a real commitment
            idealism combined with a little bloodthirstiness

    bloodthirsty idealists have started a great many wars & fought
        them too

                  bloodthirsty people won't end war or change the
                                world
and merely overthrowing governments in favor of new govts is
            frivolous   in my opinion
        it'll be interesting to talk with everyone when they
                    get back

searching, searching for something higher...
          the music strains toward transcendence
                     how sad if I shouldn't get there
                     this book must not end falling back on itself

     but tho I push and push we're not getting through
               just staying here, and it's nice
           nice is only nice for a breather--where's the action?
               my mind, my body, my soul
                     want to be stimulated

I'm a precision instrument, I operate at high energy
          too much low energy use dulls my edges
      clots my tubing
               I want to feel alive in every muscle

                              ("you know that it would be untrue
                               you know that I would be a liar")

I wonder what this book means to all the people who haven't heard
  all the songs that run through my head
                         something good I hope
     I don't care what it means to anyone
               as long as it feels nice
                     as long as it changes you

CHANGE! Talking with Raymond coming back from Montague I rapped
about land reform in Vietnam, the housing shortage & economic situation in the USA, the times soon to come when people will be fighting
for a place to live other than a high-rise and many will be
trapped in the cities because land prices will have risen so high
that only the very rich or those with a lot of self-confidence
and the ability to hang loose will even dare go looking for a new home
new place to live the rest will be cornered rats if the cities
get worse, which seems inevitable at the moment but who knows
          they'll probably get worse but myabe it won't last long
     wonder what life'll be like after the plague?
Anyway it occurred to me that the history of the next few years
especially more so than usually will be of a people simultaneously
afraid of change and demanding change
the average American's life will get worse & worse and he'll be
desperate for things to be different, be better
and all sorts of "unions" will form   demanding various sorts of change
  and people will fear & (in order to disguise their fear) hate
  because all the change that will be going on, partly as a reult
     of their own demands & needs,
   will freak them out
          caught in the transition
unable/unwilling to stick with & believe in the old
     unable/unwilling to adapt, flow with the new

                         many people will be torn apart
     it's happening here right now

if you don't know how to swim or when to float   you'll go under

eleven

        I ~~want~~ to be with Dale right now
         instead I am alone at the typewriter
        Peter came home this evening so I'm staying in Ray's room
         why am I not where I want to be?

        (I stood before Dale's door but could not knock)

        let's ask the I Ching   why am I not?

            (it could tell me: a) timing
                              b) lack of courage/ability to speak yr mind
                              c) she doesn't want you (but what does that mean?)
        does anyone not want anyone?
          or have they just missed connections?

        dig in my pocket for three coins

        nickels   nine in the first/seven/seven (heaven to wind) (creative to gentle)
            eight/seven/seven   (the gentle, penetrating)
                looks like it's going to be all right; gentle is always good advice
          when the time is right

        the reading (yes I guessed it; I am getting to know them well):
                Taming Power of the Small to The Gentle (The Penetrating, Wind)

        dense clouds no rain   success   strong element held in leash by a weak el
        (temporarily) only thru gentleness can this have a successful outcome
                (and then that's underlined by the 2nd hexagram--certainly a clear reading)

        the moment for action not yet arrived   determination within, adaptab/ility without
        9 at the beginning: return to the way how could there be blame in this? good fortune
                stay tuned folks; maybe soon we'll know what that means

        (we'll be together when the time is right)

        about Dale: I really want to be closer to her
                to her body, yes; I want to know her touch
                        and laugh   intimacy
            and to her mind; her drawings draw me   what is a person? only
            what you perceive of him since I left my glasses, I must get close
            to people to see them   Dale I want to get close to you
            however I can
            it hasn't really happened naturally that makes me uneasy fear of
            rejection but that's out, like guilt--no one can be rejected
            I might think I am; that's something else   Venus in Cancer
            but the thing is
            there are people whom I naturally, easily grow close with
            with others, the distance between us
                    or inability to communicate   is greater
            one tends to feel: well, I don't want her anyway
            sour grapes better to try harder for what is less easily reached
            some people of course prefer the difficult
            that seems strange to me too
          I like people I like ladies (and trees)   I like those who are near
            to touch   and those who are distant   the fact is, naturally, I have
            spent more time gotten to know better the girls who most immediately
            attract & are attracted by me   so it makes a weird kind of sense
            that as I become more conscious, less timid, more myself in some ways
            I want to get to know some things I've passed over so far
            I want to love some souls I've never met before   hello

An interesting day, so far   slept alone last night and woke up a lot--
I realized it was the first time in two months (since the trip to Canada)
that I've slept alone   that surprised me   Verandah and I went to a
neighbor's house to use the phone   I called Susan at Dutton--galleys in
two weeks   she may come up here this weekend (today is Monday)--Raymond
invited her--I probably won't be here, I'm going to Boston Thurs and then
probably to Arkansas (to rescue Carolanne's friend Sue from Vista)
Verandah Dale Peter Pepper and I walked down to the mailbox (2 miles)
Pepper walking fast, Peter & V slow Dale & me just right so we talked a lot
I'm learning a lot about the way things are around here from Dale
  talking to Ray and Verandah hasn't told me quite as much
Dale told me about how the farming went last summer   no one had really
farmed before (backyard gardens) so Marty got a lot of books from the
library on organic farming, composting etc etc   figured out how to do it
and told people what to do   pouring a huge amount of energy into it himself
more than anyone else could (or did)   saving the harder & more interesting
jobs for himself   which caused resentment   since Marty was usually the only
one who really knew what was going on   which is a familiar story to me,
I've done the same sort of thing more than once   at the time it always seems
like the only way to do it   but it is wasteful of human energy   Marty's
changed a lot, next summer will be different and higher
    no doubt Dale & everybody else have learned more too   not just about
gardening, but about working with people   human energy   it's the most important
field of knowledge   and there's stuff to be learned every day

Dale and I walked back   she has a bad cough; when she gets into coughing I
really want to help; of course I don't know how   is it enough just to care?
often it's all you can do   of course you have to let the other person know
you care   which is often not as easy as it looks
    my arm around her sometimes while walking
          I feel like a timid teenager!   but why not? I'm who I was then
          as well as lots of other stuff

back in the house   I showed her page eleven   she didn't say anything
 return to the way   we talked about how Ray and Veradah both are into a
lot of travelling   because not enough is happening here to hold their attention
 and not much is happening because they're never here, that is, the family's
 never together   a vicious circle   I told of my need to function at
high energy   my desire for things to happen so I could participate, be
 but my hesitancy about trying to cause things, since I am an outsider and
if you push too hard people get bugged and defensive etc   so I'm caught
below threshold   wondering what to do   I knew Ray really wants to interact
with me   and my family & his   when he visited us in Mendocino (many pages
back there) I felt that he really needed to crash in a supportive environment
so encouraged him to do that for a while   and then when he might have been
ready to get involved in stuff   Michael & he drove down to The City for a
dinner engagement with someone   promising to come back the next day   and of
course not returning   except to pass thru, by which time I was in the East
    so we didn't get together much there, and it also developed that we have
another chance   since I'm now on the East Coast and have to be while I wait for
galleys   but even tho the I'm now at Ray's home, in his room   he isn't here
he won't hold still   wants to rush off to Montreal insearch of adventure   but
 can't quite be coaxed into taking LSD here and now   he's a very strong
person, his strength is his charm and cleverness   he invites you to change
him, get close to him   but his cleverness, in service to his fear of change,
enables him to be elusive   and you can't quite hit him over the head because
he's so nice   to be with Raymond is to see him outsmart himself 12 times a day
    he needs help from his friends to get anywhere
                    like all of us   am I strong enough/friend enough to do it?

to do what?   god, what a strange situation   I really don't know what to do
 I guess the main thing is to stick with it   I wish I wasn't going to Boston
Thursday or Arkansas but we'll see what happens

I chopped some wood   Dale told me she read the first 4 pages   of this
Packer Corners section of Time Between she found them "vague" alas, it's true
I'm only too aware of the shortcomings of this new effort but I'm trying to do
what I think is right which is, keep going till it gets so good that all of
this becomes good too   don't throw this stuff away, because that would be to
say that the book can't go any further and we can't go any further   not this
month anyway <u>which is not true!</u>   perseverance furthers
        but it's hard   oh that dreadful effort & confusion   before breakthru
             the doubt: what if we don't break through?
is talking about it bad luck?
            I don't care: higher consciousness at any cost
        I think I'll go eat dinner

Dale also objected to my saying I was an observer   I think she misunderstood
I explained that I only write about what happens to me   so I'm always a part
of it not dispassionate   the people who I also can't tolerate are the people
who pretend to observe objectively/   reporters   like generals, putting others
in the front lines   to be fired upon   commanding from the rear
            I believe I can do whatever I want to do
                    including involve the people here (my family here) in this book
 as long as I put myself on the line
        take responsibility for my actions, in other words   stand up & draw fire
I would be criminal indeed if I attempted to make other lives more real (less
protected) meanwhile clutching my own safe anonymity   or hiding behind guards,
whether human (hell's angels "protecting" the Stones who had attracted others to
the same dangerous situation--without protection for the others) or otherwise--
money is a protection, a security   so is fame
       my friends   (& friends are people who will stand by you) !
       I beg you--strip me of any security--possessions--I may have
       and know in doing so you are assuming all the more responsibility for
                   my well-being
 no I do not wish to write a book in which the author is observer
        author must be protagonist, & if he wants to kill his characters at the end
            he should be prepared to die

my books all have happy endings   well I hope they will   so far so good
             higher and higher   and no end in sight

and if I don't know what's happening sometimes   well that's the price of freedom

another point: I can talk about you in these pages/ so by all rights you should
be able to talk about me   you who read these words in manuscript, feel free
 whatever you write I'll print   you would do me grave injustice not to
attack me when you want to   leaving it instead to your subconscious to do the
                          dirty work
the truth is never dirty   speak your mind
                you will anyway sooner or later/may as well be here in the open

Dale told me about "cabin fever"   people sit around reading newspapers, listless,
not noticing each other, diddling away the hours   stuck at low energy
 it happens a lot here in the winter   what can we do about it? she didn't
know   I don't know but mentioning it to each other is a first step
                  we can make it if we try

Good morning, all!   A quick roundup of the story to date, starting with locale:

Act 1 takes place in Mendocino, California, out in the woods (surrounded by
State Forest and Union Lumber Company/Boise Cascade land) about three miles
from town & the ocean/ many trees, especially redwood & manzanita, firs and
pines, rhododendrons but you don't notice them in the winter/ some rain,
but less than usual for the season/ the scene shifts continually during the
first act, day into day, starting in late December 1969 and continuing into
year one--but the location of the scene never shifts, except within the com-
pound: Paul & Carol's room, Lark's room, outdoors, the woods, the river, trip
by car to Albion, some moments at the Free School in town, the main house,
kitchen, Ron & Kay's bus etc/ the entire act takes place in Capricorn/

Act 2 takes place in [Cap. and] Aquarius, year one/ the first scene is at Tom & Pat's in
Berkeley; then Bob & Marge's in SF/ FJ's place in Berkeley, visiting our
friend Michael/ my mother's apartment on Concord Ave in Cambridge/ the family
farm in Montague (scene actually starts at Wendell), western Mass/ Sally's
apartment in Cambridge/ my mother's place again/ Dave & Pat's (Bard Hall,
where I used to live) and various subways in NYC/ Jesse & Corinne's huge house
in Bennington/ and that's all folks

Act 3 is now going on/ we're in Aquarius, verging on Pisces   (I believe today
is Feb 10 by the old calendar)/ the action takes place on a farm in Vermont/

if you stay tuned we may have a roundup of characters; meanwhile---

Dale is one hell of a lady/ last night we finally got together (at least a
lot more than before; there's always further to go, hooray!), after dinner,
after I read aloud to the family the first 20 pages of Time Between, after Dale
& Verandah & I did a lot of good sitting around (Verandah read much of "Adventures in the Skin Trade"; delightful stuff, delightful reading) and D&V read
the last thirteen pages of TB---   Verandah finishes, gets up, announces she's
going to bed (with Jeffrey who she's known 7 years) and embraces me, saying
"thank you for caring about us" and I'm really moved and happy   sitting in
green easy chair resting head in the palm of one hand my face can't be seen
so I'm not self-conscious as Dale reads finishes sits for a moment (I want
to look up but I don't) gets up I look up she right in front of me suddenly
smoothly embracing me, embracing each other, she's in my lap, she's holding
me unbelievably tight very strong I'm in happy shock hugging and hugging
I never knew this would happen   hoping, guessing, has no relation to knowing
the only joy is breakthru and the only pain is separation loving a lot in the
living room chair then into the Green Room long hours of touching and coming
and snuggling
            perhaps no one thinks I should write about this, but I think we
should not write or talk at all if we can only talk about low-energy, less
real stuff am I only allowed to write about what happens in my head? but
what happens in my world is much more beautiful---
                                   we were more than happy

I woke up (Barf-Barf jumping on the bed) alone
                              surprises

tried to change to electric but the IBM in the attic doesn't work

Jeffrey (Verandah's guest) really gets on my nerves; but it's all right;
     what I wonder is: does he <u>want</u> to bug people?

 I know I bug Pepper but I really don't want to; I think (& hope) that'll
be worked out soon/

I don't give a damn what happens to Jeffrey/

 that's how it feels right now, anyway/ I moved Ray's typer into the living room
               we're all in this thing together

                              *

I've been telling Dale my thoughts on the world-saviour bit/ It bugs Pepper
 to overhear because she lived on the edge of Fort Hill once (the left in NY)
and apparently had a bad time with some of Mel's disciples--the Karma Squad
(which I've heard of but knew nothing about; sounds like fascisti)   but my
rap on Mel & world-saviours in general is not a disciple's rap   as Wayne
(Hansen) has always (bitterly)suspected, I consider myself Mel's equal
               it's a hard gig to maintain, but it's the only way to deal with Him

A world-saviour is someone who commits himself to saving the world
          (i e the human race and hopefully all life, whatever you think that is)
        (and all individuals insofar as they are aware that their destiny is inextricably
           a part of the race's destiny--but he ain't out to "save" individuals if
        that "salvation" doesn't contribute directly to the rising of the level of the whole
             fucking thing)

A world-saviour is a strong man who has reached the point where he sort of knows
     he can make it alone   and then throws himself open to all men   on the
  grounds that if he can make it, anyone who can deal with him on his level can
     make it too   and if we all come up to his level, the world'll be a higher place

a world-saviour is a strong man who willfully makes himself more vulnerable
          not to suffer our sins for us
          but to suffer our pains <u>with</u> us
     and let his strength inspire & strengthen our own
          I like the word "strength" but "faith" is okay too

In his book (written in minus 4 or 5) <u>Autobiography</u> <u>of</u> <u>a</u> <u>World</u> <u>Saviour</u> Mel tells
a little parable about how he was sent here from another planet--Earth was orig-
inally an experiment to see how low the vibration level of spirit could go/ But
they (the experimenters) lost control and couldn't raise the level back to normal/
so Mel (the latest in a line of several) was sent to Earth to be born here and
grew and sound his note--see, his note being higher it would attract people and
make 'em yearn for a higher state/ and Mel would have to do everything he could to
get to a higher place, because being caught in the earth's low vibration would be
like suffocation for his spirit/ and since he's buried in the earth (its people)
he can't get out/get higher without bringing the whole damn thing with him/ so
he's a world-saviour cause he has no choice/ he's in pain/ and he just sounds his
note and it just strives endlessly to get higher, back to where we once belonged,
          be free

                         and that's a nice story, which he wrote for some
                         friends of his, & then expanded till eventually it
                         was a book saying what he had to say   but thinking
                         up a clever story doesn't make you a world-saviour

so many things about Dale blew my mind
   things I didn't know or even begin to understand
   until we made love last night

she's incredibly strong--in a woman of another temperament it would be scary
(to me)   but I knew (not just consciously but deep inside) with Dale that she
doesn't want to swallow me or snuff me out she's just holding on tight
 affection   it feels really good   I'm sure I've never slept with a girl
so physically strong   energetic   bear hugs but not like wrestling
   (I was a varsity wrestler in high school)   no competition
            her bit is to be independent

and that's fascinating too   I'm sure it's why I woke up alone this morning
it made me feel funny   I'd been having a very intense dream   starring Jann
Wenner and Carolanne and some others   and me having stolen some ms or something
Jann and the author wanted but I had good reasons for what I'd done   I was quite
unpleasantly righteous & Carolanne was mad at me   we went up and down elevators
outsmarting our pursuers hiding   that's all I remember   anyway when I saw
Dale wasn't there I wondered if she'd got up early   seemed unlikely; we were both
exhausted   the door was open thru the bathroom to her room   I looked and there
she was in her own bed   I went back to mine (Ray's) wondering if I'd done something
wrong after all I'd been pretty unpleasant in my dream   maybe I took all the covers
who the fuck knows? but it's not hard to make me wonder about things like that
 I didn't want to wake her, knowing how tired I was myself   and not wanting to
make a big thing out of it   later when I was ready to get up (I slept and woke
a number of times--in one dream we were in a buffet restaurant, rapping with some
very famous person who was about 50, fat and with his head shaved working as a
Buddhist monk/manservant for some other cat   writing children's books for E P
Dutton under a psedonym the food was good Bob Dylan came in wearing four cowboy
hats said hello to me   he was very pushy, obnoxious, talking about money   I
called him on it we grinned at each other, doing the spade "hit me" hand bit)
I did go in to her room; she was awake   lying in bed I wore the bottoms of my
long underwear   asked why she left she didn't say much but I knew then it wasn't
anything I'd done   and that made me realize it was a way of asserting her independence
     Aries independent

I crawled into bed with her   we snuggled and talked but didn't actually fuck
because that was part of her independence thing, you dig?   so I didn't force it
probably couldn't have   game-playing in a way but we can both dig it   it's just
a way of communicating   as long as you knew you knew----   we talked about independence   I said I was also into interdependence, making myself dependent on
others 'cause I want to be & to make it easier for them to depend on me the fact
is I need it I need my friends & family   anyway she said maybe she was too independent   others here aren't on the same trip; I think she was saying she hasn't
gotten into a shared dependence with individuals here really   tho she's very much
loved & part of the family   we get what we need if we let it happen
      what do we need?

                              attention & affection----   ?

this interaction (need a better word, fast) with Dale is really mind-expanding for me
   she's in many ways very different from most of the people I knew   and still _real_
so my range of awareness of who people are is being expanded   it's exciting & fun
            a good trip

In <u>Pushing Upward</u> I rapped with Mel about how he wrote <u>Autobiography</u>:
                    "At that time I dreaded putting that title on it,
                    cause I didn't want the responsibility that goes
                    along with calling myself a world-saviour/ At
                    that time/ I just didn't want to have to be that
                    for people/ But somehow, somehow I had to call it
                    that/ cause it was true"
and see, for me, the moment at which Mel became a world-saviour--for better
or worse; if you want to make judgments that's your gig; I'm not interested
in <u>how</u> <u>good</u> a performance a w-s seems to put on, as long as I'm convinced he's
a brother, he's really committed, he's doing it--was the moment he announced
it, when he put that title on the book, when he said: that parable I told you,
that was about me   I'm going to do it, I'm doing it   it's true, it's actually true of all of us   but it's when we realize it, become aware and accept,
embrace, the responsibility   that the term "world-saviour" applies
it's a commitment   when Ray said "know that you need only ask, I will
never refuse" he was committing himself publicly to a thing that is utterly
out of his control for better or worse he has to live up to his commitment to
the world   whatever he thinks it is   he has to be himself, he's gone so far as
to announce that he is who he obviously is, that he knows it, and so he really
can't being an aware & strong cat squirm out of it now he's thrown himself
in the water & he's going to learn to swim

                                        that's the commitment

okay: it's long overdue but I'll say it clear now: I'm a world-saviour too

            I dunno but I think my gig is to tell the truth in public

        and to give strength to my friends

                    care for my family

                the usual stuff

                        god, it really is hard to face it

    responsibility   commitment   a gig like this is a gig for life

                            fortunately it's a hell of a lot of fun

once you accept that you can't back out

                (after all, if the only joy is breakthru
                 we might as well set about the business of breaking through,
                                getting higher,
                 if we hope to find some joy in our lives)

                            glad I'm in the band

eighteen

"you get what you need" is an expression of faith

                    and if that surprises you, coming from the Rolling Stones
          then you don't know the Stones
                    listen
   " but it's all right now, in fact it's a gas
     I'm Jumping Jack Flash, it's a gas gas gas! "   that energy comes from faith

                    and it's always justified

                    /oh happy day/

you don't have to call it god, but you still have to trust in god you know
     whether god is the universe or yourself   or someone in between

   "you don't have to come down"
                              that applies if you're tripping or if you 're Jesus
                                             or both

stay high, baby
if you need help, ask for it

we've reached a kind of plateau here: I've been building up to that announcement
for so long but now it's just an afterthot, a year ago I said I was a prophet,
which is the same telling-the-truth-in-public bit, and I've talked about world-
saving so often and in such a way as to make it obvious that that was what I
was about earlier in this book I invited people who are not afraid of me to be
with me if they can be on my level/whatever that is   that's the kind of open,
public gig   expression of vulnerability that I identify with world-saviours
and I've always sort of assumed that's who I was   why, just a few pages back I
said I was equal to Mel (the different of course; we all are different, more so
than anyone realizes)   but now I've finally made the announcement   the public
commitment   big fucking deal I wonder what's for dinner?

I'm set free to find a new illusion
 god, I wish we had a copy of that Velvet Underground album here
   "Oh Happy Day" was such a flash
     things really were high last spring
  when we get through the surface confusion
    they can only be higher now

life! life!
you don't have to come down!

(thank you Sly)

I want to take you higher---

nineteen

I have faith that, even tho it's still not clear by any means, things are really
getting high around here   and in general are getting better all the time
     Altamont not down from Woodstock but a plateau, part of the development of
  consciousness that is slowly bringing us to the next stage
          which will include some central image much higher than Woodstock
               as Wdstock was higher (felt just as good, but further along)
               than the first San Francisco & NY be-ins
                    Chicago helped pull us thru to Wdstock
                    that's how it works
     (one should also mention the Pentagon, Monterey, etc etc but this isn't a history)

anyway, bearing in mind that on the overview things are getting better
I'd like to introduce an item from today's Boston Globe
(this recreant household still gets newspapers):

(front page lead story)   Hunt Widened for Oil Source off Vineyard

               "The Coast Guard yesterday stepped up an effort
               to determine the source of a mysterious oil slick
               that drifted ashore here and has killed hundreds
               of wild birds"   (and then this fantastic picture
of some guy standing before rows and rows and rows of dead birds--looks like
some fantastic traffic jam on a sixteen-lane freeway--
                         and where do you think the demand for that oil
               comes from, anyway?

yes folks, this is another attempt to get you to feel bad about your lovable
old automobile, which is the very thing that consumes so much of that oil that you
see rolling up on your beaches up and down the Atlantic and Pacific coasts
               if there was no demand for the stuff they wouldn't keep drilling for
it and shipping it
                         anyone driving a fossil-fuels burning vehicle
                              or heating his home with oil heat
                              is a criminal
     yes it's true many of us are criminals
               and it's nothing to feel romantic about, it's not like being an outlaw
     criminals of this sort are very much within the good old law
               the only thing to do is to STOP IT
               as much as you can today and a little more tomorrow
          don't let yourself off easy   maybe you can't give up your car today
                              but you can start using it less
                              you can strt thinking about giving it up
     never mind putting pressure on someone else (by writing letters hah hah)
          to develop a cleaner car
                    hell, highways aren't too good for the planet either
          and the only one who can affect the world is the only person in it who is real
                              <u>YOU</u>
so how about thinking about it? (from page 6 of the same paper):

     Nova Scotia Slick Killing Sea Birds
     "Anti-pollution crews, under government directive to destroy a shattered
     tanker and the oil it is spilling into the North Atlantic, said yesterday
     their greatest problem would be how to ignite the thick globs of heavy Grade
     C oil/
     "The oil slick spreading from the tanker Arrow, owned by Greek shipping
     magnate Aristotle Onassis, snaked into the North Atlantic, breaking into
     smaller globs and depositing dead sea birds along the shores "

meanwhile the guys at Wendell want to open a gas station!   criminals twenty

       Things are getting better but they're also getting worse/
       That's because there's two things happening/
       The old age is coming to an end
       The new era is beginning
       And we poor mortals are caught in the crunch
                    but it's fun
                    if you're strong
                    if you're not you'd better work on it

       Time between--- and it's pretty much up to us
                whether we choose to see things as getting better
                                        or getting worse
                  cause both are true   paranoia is true perception
                      but in the end the change is going to happen
            if you envision apocalypse maybe it's because you're going to die
         if we see a beautiful new world beginning to happen
                         maybe it's because we're going to live

which side are you on?

I sure am writing a lot today
high energy breeds high energy

the closer people are the more they can give each other

it takes a world-saviour to give people the courage to let go of their chains

   have
I/saved the world & it's saved me
                                more times than I can count

             I'd like to thank all the people who love each other

the only real high is high energy, awareness
                     intensity, interaction
          oh, and closeness
                 smoothness
                     the way things feel when they're going right
           they can be very relaxed
               relaxing is a part of high energy functioning
       you can let go--the important thing is not to slow down

I'm surrounded by animals: Barf-Barf the border collie, Beanie the bunny
        Mamoushka the white bitch goddess   Pippi la Peche another (puppy) bitch
     cats of various stripes: Needle, Mother Honeywell, Percy, Packer & Grey Kitty
        let me tell you, animals are a good thing to be surrounded by

               better than oil slicks

(oh, I forget Rosemary, the goat, who's outside, and Janice the horse in the barn
                with several chickens)

twenty-one

It's been raining for many hours now/ The snow's all washed away from above
the ice and it's hard to walk out there/ (This is PETER speaking)

     I just want to tell the people that I've put a kerosene lamp up in
     my room; Evann (very soft) gave it to me/ I had asked her if she
     had one--
               "Yes" she said
                Yes?
               "Yes I have two and

it's up in my room now; I can unscrew the dim electric bulb and sit in the rocker
way after dark and work on my novel which is called
                    BURNT TOAST, a fiction,
               started on the last day of the last year,
                 it's about sitting still on the farm
                    till the outlines of things fall
                                        away/
                         (It's a love story)
          In the early
          afternoon
          today, a girl said that the devil was chasing her, and I said I knew
                    a spell or two; she should try this one:
                    All evils of life vanish
                    for he who keeps the sun in his heart/
     And later
               when I'd finished writing for the day I blew out the kerosene
               lamp and put some more wood in the stove and crossed to the
               big house/Three
                         new leaks have opened in the reef since
                         last night
               I just want to say (this is still Peter talking)
          that
               it's nice to know I can go to bed at my
               usual ten or eleven (everyone's still
               sitting in the living room) and be sure
               that
               in the morning, after I've wakened, and
               walked, and written some pages, I can
               go into the big house and read all that
               happened, while I was asleep, in
                                        Paul's Book
                    Burnt Toast is about
                    many things, but it's not about what happened
                    while I was asleep last night

Dear Raymond:

Here it is Wednesday & we miss you, so here's a little note to tell you
what's happening   at your home/

                                                      doubting themases
Michael had 102° fever last night, forcing those/who thought his illness
psychosomatic to reclassify it psychogenic (if I got my terminology right)/
He's gone to see the doctor in Brattleboro, with Pepper; Jeffrey went along,
not exactly voluntarily, in order to catch a bus in Brat--it was unanimously
agreed that he was too much of a strain on the energy flow/no one could stand
him any more/   If you can't give you get taken away/   Peter's gone to Deerfield
or Greenfield or one of those places to get his car; then on to Montague where
he'll visit with all, especially Evann, and retrieve Verandy, who spent the
night there (leaving us with Jeffrey; two demerits)/ Bob at work, Connie at
 school/ Dale in Peter's garden apt reading Burnt Toast/ dogs rabbits & cats
here with me/

I put on a tape marked "Blonde on Blonde" but get Supersession instead/
Burned again/   Al Kooper is singing about how horrible it is (maybe it's
Mike Bloomfield) to love two women ("A Man's Temptation")/ What bullshit/

God, I can't remember any of the stuff I wanted to say to you/ if you were
here right now it'd probably be even harder to come to the point/ people
here--especially Dale & Verandah--talk about you a lot when you're not here/
your personality is obviously a key part of what holds this family together/
as we lay in your bed, Dale told me about the ritual that used to happen around
getting you up in the morning/ or afternoon/ you couldn't be woken before the
mail came of course/ there had to be a hot cup of coffee, cigarette, glass of
 water in case you wanted that/ someone would come and talk to you, trying to
get you to open yr eyes/ gentle rapping, with comments thrown in like "and then
the outhouse burned down" to catch yr attention/ Barf-Barf up on the bed/ the mail
presented, bills on the bottom/ good letters you would read out loud/ talk about
the planned activities for this day/ I can't capture the spirit of it, but it
sounds like a beautiful celebration/ you'd sure be crazy to go to Hollywood/
can't get that kind of service there/ I've been told (with demonstrations) of
 how you sing "Would You Like to Swing on a Star?" and "Ireland"/ I mention this
because it's the sort of thing that's mentioned to me/ and tho I haven't got
 the feeling of it in my words now, I could certainly feel the delight of it all/
talking with the family/ everyone loves you
     but where are you? California, Boston, Montreal? people here are out of
touch with you/   and with each other/ Verandah sleeps at Montague, the Baby Farm,
spends the day at Hannons'/ anywhere but here/ you tell me nothing's happening
& people aren't together 'cause it's winter/ is that the reason?   does it have to
be this way? I don't know why I'm asking these questions/ I'm not with my family
either/ but I am/   where are we?

We talked (Dale & I) about your Writing Career/ You put together an anthology
of stuff from LNS to sell to a publisher to get some money to help meet the mortgage/
no one was interested/ Beacon Press said: we don't want this, but Wd you write a book
yrself about yr experiences with LNS? Send us 2 chapters & an outline/ You were
flattered, need the bread; wrote two chapters & got a contract/ but you didn't really
want to write the book/ so much work to dredge up all that stuff from the past/
didn't write anything for three months/ then forced it all out, like going to Cambridge
to work in the bank/ got to meet the mortgage

Dale's telling me this, & I'm relating it to what you told me a few days ago:
something about how writing's not fun for you the way it is for me/   such
bullshit/ like the bit about things not being so "advanced" here/ it's easy
to say things are impossible/ but it's never true

     Well of course writing's no fun for you (except letters, as you said):
you're a wage slave/ you're writing <u>for</u> E P Dutton, Beacon Press, the Atlantic
Monthly, the literary critics, all these clowns/ you know you're a better writer
than 99% of th creeps, so you're just <u>showing</u> you're a better writer/ instead of
forgetting all that nonsense and getting to work on what has to be done, what
you need, what you want/   oh yes, you have a good excuse--you have to provide
for your family bring home the bacon and you <u>know</u> They won't <u>buy</u> the stuff
you would write if you really let go cause they wouldn't understand it, no one
would but you and yr loved ones but why deal with anyone who isn't (at least
potentially) a loved one?   to get bread, of course

       who's to say what "providing for the family" entails? the family needs you
here they need you happy   maybe what has to be done is not to get enough
money but to make money unnecessary except perhaps for the trickle that comes in
effortlessly   how can it be done? well I don't exactly know,
but if you try sometime----   it's a matter of faith

     And that's why it's inexcusable to write anything but what gives you pleasure,
what fills your need/   Using the family as an excuse/ Because your family wants
you to write the truth, wants you to do what's right, much more than they want you
to pay the mortgage/ and <u>it's a matter of faith</u> that the better and truer your
writing is, the better that'll be for your family   in every way

     Your essay in the last Occasional Drop is the best piece of writing I've read
by you, I've told you that before, I don't know if you believed me/ I read it to
Dale last night, she really liked it, she read it before in Santa Fe but didn't
really register then; if your writing is just going to/pretty & clever then maybe
people will appreciate its pretty cleverness first time through every time (if
they give a shit) but if you're actually talking about what's real to you then
you'll have to be a little more patient with your readers & maybe you won't have
as many readers at first but the people who care will get there----
                                                      Naturally being
on the farm and having Dale's annotation I "understood" (dug the references) about
seven times as much of what you said as the first few times I read it, but it seemed
great to me back then nevertheless/

     Dig it, who understands a Dylan song or a Stones song the first few times or
"understands" it in its entirety <u>ever</u>? who cares? are you interested in being as
good as John Updike, or as good as Dylan? I mean, what's happening in your writing, in my
writing, is the music, the immediate impact, and the impact you get the second time, etc;
it's never the "meaning," sure there's some kind of cognitive strain running through
our raps because that's the way we use words, that's the form we're into but it's
doesn't matter what we're <u>saying</u>, you even suggested that in your Drop essay---- so
is the stuff worthless? hell no, it's the sound, the feeling of the stuff that makes
it, the communication that happens when you look at someone, regardless of what
you look like----

     Well okay, you know all this: so how can you pretend that writing isn't fun, isn't
satisfying? Is it in any way different from picking up an instrument and making music?
Has anyone yet suggested that making music, real music, hitting a drum or singing out
yr heart or whatever you do, has anyone suggested that that's unreal, ego-tripping?
Who would dare? Well don't you think you're a musician?
                                   Aren't we all?   let's do it---

So much for writing to Raymond--oh, I could say more but there's time for that;
meanwhile I want to try to get this thing together   this book I mean

I'm supposed to see Sam Lawrence tomorrow (Thurs) I think-- which means going
to Boston, & then Arkansas after that, and that's all fine but the truth is I
don't want to leave here at all right now   I wish Raymond would come home with
Carolanne and Jimmy this very night, and then we could all get together
                    and think about what happens next

   as it is it's all so lumpy   coming & going   towards & away from
                   just imagine us all sitting here together here
                            no it's too much to ask for
I miss Carolanne
that is, I want to be in touch with her   I don't mind our being apart but
I like to know where she is   how she feels
I hope to call her tonight, if it's not too late when we finish dinner
which we're about to start
thank god there's always dinner

when Ray was at Caladan he said it was exactly like Packer Corners
meaning the feeling of the people & the situation I think
but whatever he meant I felt he was right
and still do
though it's totally different of course
that's why this book can now happen here instead of returning to where
it started
'Cause it's all the same   as they say here   something noted on an acid trip
so many things here date from particular family acid trips
it's nice; gives some order to the mythology
we need another acid trip
I hope they bring some back with them; I don't have enough
and I haven't taken what I have 'cause we shd all take it together
it isn't me or anyone who needs to go thru changes but us together
change the gestalt
grow closer
I hope Carolanne & Raymond have grown closer
if not Ray's a fool
 I think   and I know he's nobody's fool
she wants to be with him   why doesn't it happen?   maybe it's happening
things are probably moving towards each other
it's just hard to see from here
especially knowing I'm to go to Boston tomorrow, and feeling I'm moving away
scatter   scatter   all in different directions
oh that would be tragedy
our destiny is gathering together
true it may be slow
but we want it now---

outside the wind is blowing
fierce from the northwest
bitter cold
we huddle together
yesterday it was rain
the dogs are restless
no long walks/the weather's rough   Barf-Barf's barely been out
   but he likes it here
   set me free

    I went over to the Hammon's and called Carolanne
She & Raymond haven't got together yet but it's not because Ray's a slacker,
really/ She was tired when they got to Boston & went right to Sally's/ Ray
gave her the address where he'd be & suggested she come meet his brother etø
But Carol took him at his word that he'd be leaving for home the next night
so didn't bother---- I told her he was probly still there & she may do something
about it yet-----
God it's funny I really am disappointed   not just 'cause I'm with Dale and
I want Carolanne to be with someone nice   but because it's such an important
part of the general getting together, I mean everyone's having trouble touching
Raymond it seems & I know Carol can do it if the situation would just allow----
            for me it's a way to get closer to Ray and to Carol too in a way
        for everyone it's a great goodness   but who knows? you just have to let
it happen   and it's not happening   and I'm leaving early in the morning for
Boston & points south   what will happen?
                                        stay tuned

now the scrabble game

stop the game!   in walked
                          Raymond Jimmy Johnny Stevie
                                with a 65 VW bus just laid on them
                        and FINE vibes
                                   the only thing they forgot was Carolanne
            not forgotten; they just didn't know how to get in touch with her
                                god's will
            it's all on the way to coming together

oh my Ray's sick but still if only Carol were here   I would be incred'bly happy
                                        all would be well
                                        all <u>will</u> be well
all <u>is</u> well   isn't it?

 Uncle Louis really came thru with the bus   the boys needed a way to get back
                            to the farm, so they went to see him---

"Bubbles" is the name of the bus

 Gramps wants his own joint   claims he's got a disease

Louis sounds beautiful   loose   our own psychedelic bus!

 I've got to get this page out of the typewriter and fall into things
 Maybe I'll just rip it out

twenty-six

The Scrabble Game:


```
          F I E N D   D
          E           E
        W E E P       C
        I             A   H
        Z E N         Y   A G E
      M E                 N
      O N                 D
  G U T S
R O P E
```


                              (Dale, me & Verandah)
                                ((interrupted))

EARLY
FEB
YEAR 1

Report from **CALADAN**

~~Had a dream~~ that we were in a bueatiful wooden rowboat at gaalley bay

~~Have~~ I earned how to brew beer better than any Ive ever tasted

~~Outragus~~ head over heels in love with Raven Caspar Moon

History

Ron was going to hitch up to Canada with Carl who I fell in love with
couldnot do it and fell apart for a week into a semi catatonic state
which only TD (the queen of psycosis could understand) [NON VERBALLY]

We've been eating lots of mussels which is about two hours of blissful
joy work made more exciting by the raging storms of the mendocino coast

Lark Tom and Judy were very tight   Lark seems to enjoy balling Judy
more than Tom she approaches all of her envolvements with great gusto
and sublime confussion
LARK CLARK IS SUPER

ANDY our toy soldier guru took 2 tabs of osley acid (the pig)
and flipped out behind self flagelation he has recovered

TD is Tami Diane now with tung in sf but do to return

Oh great excitment a three year old kiddie from table mountain ranch
was lost in the woods and for two days hundreds of freaks the prisoners
the straight the heat we all combed the nooks and creaveses of Albion ridge

AND VICTORY WAS OURS WE FOUND THE CHILD TIME OF GREAT REJOICING

RICKHARDT stayed in Donalds house (the high house) for two or three weeks
taught me how to brew really great beer I'm interrupting the missive to put
aside a bottle for you right now....He is taking over Caladan when we leave
talked and liked a nd shook hands with Bill Ames

David Lakish is coming with us

Kay has the intellectual power of Strider but can draw better than TD or
Cheril Bowers and is semi fuctional at this point

As i was reading a PK Dick book the other night Judy Breagen
came in and I reciprocated and we hatched plans for going to
mexico in her new vw camper AND it made us feel very warm
we both have colds.Lark Clark has been with cold for a week
and Dr Robinson said ' lots of fucking cast the I CHING a nd
do alot of dope.Lark Clark knocked me out REALLY GOOD FUN
I really want you CAROL ANN

Lark Clark'S friend Neal a jewish ny comedian and one of the funnist
people alive is living in your cabin here at caladan and keeping it
quite warm I hope he's still here when you come back.

Love and a handshake......
alan

who am I?

back in Cambridge with Carolanne
she & George (friend from last summer) made love last night
& that made her feel better about me & Dale
but it makes her feel funny that it made her feel better
transition
someday/soon we'll be at the stage
where we'll love each other when we feel like it & because we like
the way it feels
& we know that's why we do it
no fancy reasons
immediacy
living in the present would find us in bed more often
with more people
& be better for the ecosystem...

see, we have to get off the economy
the growth-oriented goods productivity consumer possessions competion economy
if we want to save the planet
as a place where stuff like us can live

'cause the goal of a growth economy
is to use stuff up
so more stuff can be   manufactured   sold   used up
do you know what the word "consume" means?

light a match to your library
fire is a consumer

Ods Bodkins is a superb comic strip that runs in the SF Chronicle
when last I saw Ods B there was a fox
(the installment was titled: What Doth It Profit A Man If He Gain the Whole World
...And It Isn't There?)
the fox said: use up the planet!
Use it up?
Sure. The Gross National Product this year is going to be one trillion dollars
With that kind of money we can buy a dozen planets!

Gross National Product is the name of the game
tv magazine radio newspaper subway billboard advertising
making you want stuff you don't need
the consumption exchange manufacture of which
is toxic to life on this planet

but what else is there to do
besides drive cars
read magazines smoke cigarettes watch television eat garbage ?

well there's walks in the woods
music-making
bread-baking
love

the rumor that Love Is Dead
                    is capitalist   propaganda
              (Portnoy's Complaint was written by a tv manufacturer)

I had a long talk with Raymond after he went to bed last night
he was exhausted from dope disease & driving
there were things I just had to say to him so I said them and maybe
he was awake enough to get some of it
talked about in the Occasional Drop where he says things are getting
so much better & worse
simultaneously
& one of these movements just has to come out on top pretty soon
well I agree except for that last part
I think they're going to get worse for quite a while yet
and better too of course
not the same things
and you vote with your life, right Ray?
so here's the ballot:
/_/things getting better   /_/things getting worse
which are you going to focus your energy on?
spend your life with?
we do have a choice you know
it's not going to be easy to reduce our life to good stuff
but there's no question we can do it
hell, we have no choice
/_/live   /_/die
is that a choice?
well Ray's friend Marshall chose to snuff himself
& my friend Don just let go
(I don't think I could drown in ten feet of water)
so what'll it be, gents?
I vote for life   Raymond?

(I don't mind chopping wood/and I don't care if the money's no good)

we can make it if we try

What I guess I want from you, Raymond, is a commitment
(you take what you need/and you leave the rest)
when I saw you last
you didn't look too well
and since I need you by my side
on the front lines
that worried me
you went to Boston
to do something or other
something you needed, brother?

Don McNeill drowned behind coffee & cigarettes &
        not respecting his commitment to his body
Marshall Bloom asphyxiated behind shame & self-indulgence &
        not respecting his commitment to his heart
Maybe There's Nothing To Be Learned
OR MAYBE WE JUST WON'T FACE WHAT'S RIGHT IN FRONT OF US!!

there's plenty to be learned

for one thing, it's about time we started leaving the rest/
and taking what we need/

for another thing, it's time to stop kidding ourselves
with comfortable easy traditional aesthetic romantic notions
        of love-hate relationships
    and "that's the way it is"
    and "that's the way it's gotta be"
because this is revolution
and to hell with hate
to heaven with the rest of us
the garden of eden is just beyond that tree
if you're so smart why ain't you happy?

When talk of revolution has gone the rounds three times
One may commit himself
And men will believe him.

That's what the I Ching said one day in May
of minus 2
when Wayne & Trina & I   took STP in Monroe
I believe it was Revolution   to The Joyous

When one's own day comes, one may create revolution.
Starting brings good fortune. No blame.
that was line 2; and then the third...
Starting brings misfortune.
Perseverance brings danger.
When talk of revolution has gone the round three times...

        Sir, I believe the time has come.
        I wonder if you'll believe me?

I want you folks to come with us to British Columbia
but I'm not asking for that
I guess I'm ashamed to ask for it
oh my god...

What's happened to this book?
Who am I talking to?
Raymond Dale Verandah Michael Pepper Jimmy Peter Connie Bob Marty Richard?
yes...
or everyone?
yes...
anyone???   no, we don't want anyone who can't live in harmony with the environment
which I think at the moment means without public utilities
gasoline anything   packaged anything
and we don't want anyone who can't be open with his family
who's afraid of his brothers   or mistrusts himself
we don't want people who cling to external security or truth
god, does that leave any of us eligible?
probably not

but need ranks want

I don't know who I need   oh anyone I guess who can love & work & breathe

I want some Montagroovians with us too
everyone who feels part of the family
cause I'm not relating to individuals but the family
Johnny 2 Steves Evann Cathy Laz Tom Laurie Stevie M's girl whose name I can't
          remember

I've got to stop making these lists! but I know no other way to tell people
              they're wanted
Caladan of course
the family around the Free School
Albion
Caspar
you know who you are

oh god I'm embarassed   you're not supposed to do this
but my gig is to talk with my friends & relations
get a feeling for what's happening & find **ways to respond to it**
what's happening is we are warriors & frontiersmen & nebbishes
(and other stuff but I'll leave it to you to tell me)
and things are getting better & worse
which means it's getting to be time for the warriors to do whatever it is they do
and time for us pioneers
to get on with the new ways of living
we can't keep dilly-dallying with the old if we're gonna do the new
somebody's got to learn how to survive
let's get to work
   if you're having trouble with yr locale I think I've found a place where we can
        get it together   (this is a private message to my tribe)
I don't address myself to the Ft. Hill people for example who I consider family
    because somehow I feel they've got a place they're comfy in...
  is this some weird ego-trip I'm on? I'm painfully self-conscious...

who are we?

should we be together?

have to be practical y'know...

god I'm being torn in half

everything's okay
schizophrenia as I understand it is a state of tension and confusion
      caused by a gap between intuitive reality and apparent reality
                    internal & external
      which tension can produce a biochemical reaction
      not unlike that triggered by LSD in some circumstances
      which might be described as the internal universe's effort to
          alter the external universe
          by means of changing its own perception (intake) of same
      or you could say that when the conflict between internal & external
          reaches a certain intensity
          the system snaps floods   overloads in some fashion
      a psychotic break would be a sudden reaction
      schizophrenia perhaps is a word to describe a more gradual process

I dunno; it's somebody else's word & I'm throwing it around as though I
          could just make it mean whatever I feel like
but that's how kids are these days

there should probably be laws
          against letting us get our hands on the language
'cause you know we'll fuck things up beyond recognition
          making it hard for future scholars
who fortunately, being computers, won't mind the strain

check out a Borges short story called "The Library of Babel"

this book is in it

my conflict over the last few pages
is between my desire to get together with certain people
and my feeling that I have to be open to everyone
  (my fear being that openness to everyone will fuck up my relationship
                  with the people I know I love)
it's like the bit Van Dyke and I used to do about discriminate/indiscriminate
my willingness to accept (& then love) many rock groups
                                            on their own terms
despite the "immaturity" (?) of those terms
his ability to always see how the stuff could be called "good"
if one abandoned certain standards
like up and down
we never talked openly about this/ just smiled at each other
played with nuances of communication
because there was nothing really to discuss
we both knew we could each see it the other way
& both knew both our universes could not get along without the other
point of view
solipsism for two players
god we had fun   I wonder where he is?

anyway I'm still playing the indiscriminate role
but my discriminating heart
interferes   Taurus is security   my game is burning bridges
(Raymond correctly identified) (another marvelously subtle--aware--thinker)
destroying my own security costantly & then letting my heart
find a better one
keeps me in motion   seeking a state of rest...

I guess I've reached the point where I'm not talking to anybody any more
future scholars will pretend to understand
my friends will know it's how it feels
not what it means
that matters
let me touch you thus
the split in this book
is author/protagonist
I get so into writing for my friends
that I forget the outside people (if there are any)
and--yes!--it's the idea (which I claim to renounce) that there are still outsiders
that makes it so confusing for me
I don't want to draw to me people I won't love
obviously the solution to that is to be completely myself
but the poor publishers have to think about "outside" readers
how will they understand?
they don't realize we can sell a hundred thousand or so
just to the people who know the characters
they don't get the bit about everybody being just five friends away
meaning there's no one I know
who isn't a friend-of-a-friend-of-a-friend-of-a-friend of yours
whoever you are
so maybe if the publishers aren't game we can just pass these things by hand

I guess that solves that

but I still need the bread to buy the boat   well if I'm supposed to have it
it'll come to me
got to keep the faith
it works you know/just as the I Ching always (so often) tells the truth
more often than anything else
the New York Times almost never tells the truth

god I feel a lot better

my external reality says you people are strangers in a bookstore
my internal intuitive says you're dear friends
who I sometimes feel like making love with
and don't have to fear telling all to
even if you don't understand you'll accept because it's me
I mean you'll say "that Paul Williams sure talks a lot of bullshit
but he's okay"
which is all anyone can ask

all I want is to get what I need
I know I can pull it off if I can just remember
that I don't always need what I think I need
faith
trust
I trust you

end of external reality
end of conflict

                              poof!

God--a lot of things I want to talk about
usually one strain emerges dominant--we'll see

just made some Instant Pudding   mix it with milk, let it sit five minutes
tastes quite good no doubt has some awful chemical to make it jell faster
we're in such a hurry   we're living on borrowed time

all the things that get us there faster--cars, jets, instant pudding--
are slowing us down on some broader scale

the perpetual motion machine can't be invented
it already exists & it's called the universe
have some respect for it

you can't beat the system
why would you want to?

"time" is a clever human invention to enable us to think we have some control

it's killing us by degrees

if we could just dig the flow   we'd be immortal

saw Sympathy for the Devil tonite   with Bhob & Paula, Carol & me
(here Bhob--this is the page you're mentioned on)
Godard called it One Plus One but the producer or somebody fucked with
his work in order to make more money
somebody's always doing that God I hate it
if they'd just let us do what we want completely we'd all be happier,
                    even the money-counters
Sam Lawrence decided he didn't want to publish Time Between, not as it
stands anyway   tho he asked me to send him the finished book (asked, not urged)
and part of the reason --he liked it at first you see-- is that he got a
discouraging report from one of his outside readers which fed his own doubts
but I think what really did it is I would walk in after ten days or so
and say: here's another forty pages   so he stopped thinking about whether
he enjoyed what he was reading and started worrying about craftsmanship
he spent some time telling me that he didn't think it possible to write good
stuff without really sweating over it, that is, rewriting and pruning etc
which I can dig I do that too   but this is a different sort of book for
this one all the editing has to be of my life I just have to be sure I'm high enough
to begin with   and honest enough and brave enough not to wander from the subject
whatever it is
I mean this is largely intuitive but isn't that how art is made?
well I guess there are lots of ways
I write many different sorts of books
because every moment is different
I know I'm doing what I have to do
anyway I really like Sam & think he has good taste
so I was disappointed especially to hear him tell me that I don't work hard enough
because I know a lot of good writers and few work as hard as I
which is not a boast the easier the writing is to do, the easier it reads
the better it is
that may not always have been true but I think it's true now
immediacy is what we all value
not aesthetic antics   and the irony is--if I'd handed Sam a finished book
he wouldn't have thot about how I did it   and I think would have really dug it

Lets's see... I was saying
they should let us do what we want
a meaningless statement--but I just mean   that if publishers producers etc
would let the really creative artists have free rein   fantastic stuff would
result   and in the long run fantastic stuff is very good for business
look at rock music for instance   immediacy saved an industry   for a few years anyway
I don't say publishing will last too much longer   since it's an old-style
        economic form   but while it does last I think more books would be sold
just as many more records in toto were sold in -2 than in -7
if they'd start printing books like this   more immediate, exciting, less training
        needed to read them   you don't have to be conscious of traditions
        to appreciate Time Between   or the Rolling Stones
maybe that's arrogant but it's what I believe
remove the distance   (immediacy=no time distance)
tear down them walls

<u>Sympathy</u> <u>for</u> <u>the</u> Devil   Godard flic featuring the Rolling Stones
black militants (?) in a junk car lot with guns & reading from books
the Stones in the studio doing repeated takes of this song   interviews
with various   narrator reading from a pulp novel with famous people
especially international political figures   as characters   delightful
everybody gets more & more relaxed as the flic goes on
at the end there's just easy-going anarchy   not tension
the movie stays on the ground watching the camera-rig fade into the distance
because there's no longer anything to shoot
it's all there
no distance
1+1 like Blonde on Blonde   adds up to one   I think
when you're in Memphis you don't got no Memphis blues

anyway it's interesting because it was during that very song
"Sympathy for the Devil"
that Meredith Hunter was stabbed & killed   at Altamont
(& they made a movie of that too)
and what's more interesting is you watch the flic and listen to the song
and Mick Jagger never gets to show off in this one, gang
not one little bit
he's just there working like anyone at work
I don't look romantic at the typewriter
and so who's the devil
who you s'posed to empathize with?
the camera looks & looks & don't find no evil & vanishes
and I do believe the same thing will happen with the Chas Manson flic
currently happening in people's heads
who's the devil?
I want to empathize with him man but I can't find him
no duality
that's cause he's already you
("why shout about who killed the Kennedys
when after all it was you & me?")
hope you guessed my name
this book was written by Charlie Manson
Sirhan Sirhan
Paul Williams .
Richard Nixon
there are no villains   just men   just man   & one + one
is Me
                    (think I'll straighten Myself out a little)

if they would let the really creative artists   have free rein
fantastic stuff would result
if they would let everyone have free rein
everyone would be really creative artists
one of the things I want to do with this book & my future ones
is get away from the idea of the artist as someone with special talent
leading a special life (or at least writing about far-out stuff)
this book is about everyday life
the parts written by non-writer friends are at least as good as what I write
and anyone who wants can sit down & write a book just as good
at least insofar as it'll be interesting to the people who matter,
the people around you
the people in it
it's like closed-circuit tv   anyone who has camera and set
can make fascinating movies
fascinating to him & his friends anyway
(when will cheap good videotape equipment be on the market?
answer: just before the market ceases to exist)
and a typewriter can be a closed-circuit tv
you don't need no editor to certify you talented
just go down to the nearest xerox machine
3¢ a page and they do it for you   in Berkeley
(hey kids! make copies of this book's pages cheap! scare the publisher!)
it's true that xerox and cassette recorders etc
will eventually rob artists (& their agents) of all royalties
but then we can live off the goodwill of the people
and the fat of the land
which is more fun & ecologically sounder
the trust economy
remind me to give you my rap on that sometime

anyway I think very soon we will all be artists
everyone who survives
and no one and nothing will be special
except for everyone   if you dig what I mean

Godard's flic is a lovely piece of music
simple and real   I sure felt relaxed at the end
if I remember right what I read somewhere, he got angry 'cause the producer
put in the final version of the song
which is a fuck-up because the point is, there is no final version
eventually there are no longer even versions
no time   or space
but it's all right   the audience scarcely notices   the intellectuals walk out
thinking   the others walk out humming   a fine flic

and I understand the song better now
maybe Mick does too
"my knife right down your throat"
what knife?

Tom I've been thinking about you tonight
I really want to be with you
I've been wondering if it's okay that I left when I did
but of course it's okay   & I know you can feel that
        from this distance I don't know how to tell you   that there's no distance
                                        between us

                    "How can I preach ecology," Godfrey
                    asked, "and sell this stuff?"
                            Colgate-Palmolive gulped
                    Nor have any of the three networks
                      "If we took every commercial off
                    the air which advertised a potential
                    pollutant," said one spokesman, "we
                    wouldn't have any commercials left
                    at all."
                              (Newsweek)

     This flash is for all the little boys & girls who think you can do
something about ecological problems by petitioning the government or
the corporations.
          Nothing can be done about the ecology   until we destroy the economy.
              We destroy the economy by abandoning it.

start abandoning it today
the goods on your shelf
        the wires in your house
                the steed you ride
                    is the enemy.

You cannot reform the world.
The world already has a form.
The word is revolution.
Molting. Form in constant change.
                              Change your life
                              roll with it
                              Don't try to change institutions
                              it is time to escape from institutions
                              shed them like skin
your life should be an analogue
of the universe you want to live in
'cause it is the universe you live in
                              you like to breathe poison?
                              you like to eat shit?
long as you have some money in your pocket?
                              but money ain't worth so much
these days...
              you are the economy
you got to stop spending money literally   if you were dropping bombs on
villages, how long would it take you to realize you were the one killing
those people?   well, you are the one killing the earth
              you think that's heavy?
              then why don't you stop?

you may be tired of ecological rants
well I'm tired of 'em too
pious pronouncements from murderers
         people who say they can't/won't change their life-style
              have my complete contempt

it may not be much but it's all I have to give them
and god bless Arthur Godfrey
him I can give my love
                  god bless all conscious men

2-16

    I've been reading the early part
of this book, just finished Tom's letter
(page 31), made me think about everyone,
touching hugging holding Tom fucking/
making love with Judy (we never have)
fucking Lark.   Seeing Lark, her breasts
shining, dark thick hair falling over
them, look up to grin on face her legs
up   me between them   excitement ec-
stacy. oh it's nice to think about.
where are my friends and lovers tonite?
(letter from Thistle: she, Lark, Yarrow,
Aeko, Alan, Neal all at Eric Matlen's
girlfriend's house in LA, maybe on to
Mexico by now... yay team! Carolanne
and I are on a Trailways bus between
Boston & NY, the Boston terminal burned
down this evening, strange smell. It's
about 2 a.m, strange city-to-city trip,
none of this seems real to meany more,
doesn't involve me, I just try to keep
cool, soon (someday) we'll be back in
Vermont Mendocino   B.C.   ...home.) I
really want to fuck my old friends tonite,
I guess that's what it means to "miss"
people. To think of them and want to be
together.
    Oh Lark dark hair and bright nipples
Judy must be wonderfully pregnant very
sexy Tom I can see/feel your face before
me smiling

(Now in NY) glasses on and off these days,
had to wear them for the movie the other
night & browsing around Bhob's apartment.
Now I'm inconsistent, my reasoning is this
is the jungle need to be aware at all
times to survive/but not wearing glasses
also very helpful in the city, less information overload all the time, walk down
the street in my own soft-edged world, re-
duces tension. And with no clear code to
follow I take them on and off with people,
alternating desire to see them in focus and
desire to relax with them, schizophrenic on
off on off likeI've been known to do on acid
trips but it's all an acid trip now.

    Since I saw David last (2 weeks ago,
at which time he read 120 pp of Time Between) he reread Stranger, first time
in many years, and got a lot out of it,
times have changed and the book just gets
clearer and better. And it made him appreciate TB more, and vice versa. I feel
funny about what I've written here "about"
Stranger in a Strange Land, I feel I
haven't been able to begin or end a thought,
just throw the middles out for grabs,
that's how it is I guess. But I have a very
simple, clear rap on Stranger when I talk
with people: it comes from what Michael
said to me about the Stones (his Ramparts
article just came out--the girls in the
office were reading it when we went for
the typer) after touring with them: they
are naive and arrogant. Not manipulators--
innocents--but not manipulated either, innocents abroad unafraid of acting, cocksure
of what they're doing never knowing what
will happen. I know the feeling. In fact
it's a gas. When you feel like you and you
do what you feel like you know it's right
you could almost swagger but you don't pretend
to know what's coming the "results" of your
actions the history of the future is inevitable unavoidable and unknowable
& as long as you're cool to the unexpected
I guess you're innocent   the Stones are innocent all I know is Michael saw it and
he's got a good eye and my ear tells me that
too but this was going to be my rap on Stranger
 oh my you see how it goes   "naive" means not
to know what's going on when Everyone Knows
what's going/ The Way Things Are "that's just
the way it is, dear"   I REJECT THAT KIND OF
TALK don't you know you don't know the way it
is? none of us knows, it's too BIG for our comprehension
anyway I know I don't know   naive and I'm
proud of it   imagine the nerve of that
Valentine Michael Smith   pretending he doesn't
know things just are the way they have to be/
such arrogance   but his strength is
he's not pretending   the Rolling Stones
know who they are   don't know who they're
gonna be   if you really don't know or tell
yourself you know what's going to happen to you
and you keep on being everything you know you are
 more all the time then thou art God
       and you're movin' on up
           (the arrogance of not knowing that
            things have to be this way is the force
            with which we change   our world)

God, forty-one pages! David G. Hartwell,
perhaps my most perceptive reader, notes
that there are pages,in the segment he
just read (121 to thirty eight),that don't
have to be where they are, that are not as
organically at home as everything that
went before. Not out of place, just homeless.
True. He cites the <u>Stranger</u> quote page and
the ecology rap on the last page he read.
I feel what he means. I mention it because
I regard it not as something I've done wrong
that I should change (it really isn't possible to make a mistake) but as an indication of what's happening, even as things are
coming together in my mind, in my book, new
stuff is happening that's moving out, that
in no way fits into what is now the mainstream.
Yes there is resolution but you can't resolve
<u>everything</u> because even as you get it all together
new stuff bursts out all over. The situation
is dynamic, it's in constant flux, it feels
good to get some order out of it sometimes but
you can't cling to that order or try to make
that order absolute, the only absolute is MORE
and the seeds of movement are present even as
you enter a state of rest. Huh? What's happening? Well what it is is I would really like to
show my craftsmanship and discipline as an
artist by rounding off the edges here and bringing it all home but I just can't do it, this is
my life and it creates itself, it can't be manipulated for the sake of an aesthetic, for the
sake of showing off some kind of cleverness or
skill. Reality is always the greatest high. I
have faith that this book will feel good in the
end, it feels pretty good to me now tho there's
some stuff I know I have to do, guess I'll just
get to work....
Those pages that seem homeless would look right
at home if you could see the total picture
   but it's too big, we can't step back that far
but you can feel it, you can feel the total picture
any time you want, you're part of it
     and you <u>are</u> it
    this universe is you
        Thou Art God   (there it goes again)

okay so I'm God & I know I'm God believe me,
it still ain't nearly enough
          and maybe one of you pretty girls
would like to come help me look for something
                higher

                    yeah that feels good...

thank you Carolanne
                          I wonder if any of you
know   just how much I love that girl
                   I just wonder if any of you do...

god this book is almost over/I'm going to miss you all

make love keep warm stay happy   wherever you may be

all that has to happen now is for me to get
back to Raymond   and Dale and Verandah and
Packer Corners   Montague

and before I can do that I have to fly to Memphis
  so Carol will know I love her
it's a pleasure, a joy to have the opportunity
  to let Carol know I love her

some go to war/some go to Arkansas
    and all a woman ever really wants   from her man
is that he be with her
           but there's always a little distance
  and that's the pain we must embrace
        as long as there is love
when we're totally together we'll have even phased out
                                            that
       (and I'm sad 'cause I think we'll be sad
              but It'll be so happy)

don't think about tomorrow/just let tomorrow be

when Don died Wayne sent me a postcard

Dear Paul: God bless tragedy & joy   (he said)
              they are all we have left.

(and Dale said she's going to embroider that
      --in his book Peter had her embroidering
   the message "It's fun to make love"
              and that's good too, oh yes
         but God bless tragedy & joy
              and I love Dale)

and this is a book in which Peter writes his book

Packer Corners   all the way to Arkansas and back
 I'll be on my way there
                   so glad to be with my family
   and always eager to get back to them
I want to be with Carolanne David & Pat   and I am
and I want to be with Alan and Carl and Lark and Tom
and Don but that one's dead oh well we'll meet again
   (I can feel it)   we always do

43

The day after my first trip with Don
we smoked a lot of pot
lost in intense and convolute thoughts
I got very scared

because I felt pain, the greatest pain I've ever known
and the pain was consciousness, and I knew
that now that I was aware of this thing I
would always be aware   and in such great pain
and that scared me

here's what I became aware of, that was so painful:
I realized the world was changing
and would change beyond recognition
I realized the children younger than us (I was almost 19)
would in this new world be creatures beyond
my comprehension

and I knew that I and my friends would be left behind
unable to abandon the only world we loved
but doomed to lose it anyway
and never quite able to be part of the new
I must have felt the pain of an entire generation
at least
it was like a plunge into water unbearably hot and cold
and no escape

44

and that was a real experience, no hallucination
and my reasoning was good, for I never did escape
                                        that path
tho I did learn to embrace it
   and that destroyed the fear, dissolved it
              the fear is the dangerous part

Don held my hand, and I tried to explain
              where I was
         and my vision of us as explorers
        who reached the mountain top
                                   and saw
           what could never be forgotten
   and the adrenalin of explaining
              to Don, who was really listening
overcame the fear
       and the joy of being able to breathe
                                      and live
the joy of breaking thru
                       balanced the path
       and you who are becoming conscious
            and read these words
         let me hold your hand
         and give you joy to ease the pain
                 of time between

Here we are in Nashville-- I hadn't planned to write any
more till we get back to Vermont...but plans are the idlest
of thoughts,
                    and here I am.

We're on our way to visit Carol's friend Sue in Marked Tree,
Arkansas--we left Bard Hall at about 12:30, arriving at JFK
just barely in time to catch American Airlines' 1:55 flight to
Memphis (stopover in Nashville). We had a good flight---the
stewardess was very nice to us and I started reading Red Planet,
Carolanne looked thru Esquire and a copy of Awake. Somewhere
along the way I started pushing at Gathering Together in my
mind, for the 100th time... the book exists at present as a
theme and a bunch of writings that seem to me to belong together... no structure yet, just some of the raw materials, and an
intuition. Anyway, something fell into place and suddenly I had
the first chapter of GT---combining a "false start" that I'd
made on my Woodstock piece, a short essay I wrote for the program
booklet of that festival, the first issue of There Must Be Some
Way Out of Here (which only in the last few days have I consid-
ered incorporating into GT) and a one-page issue of Friends &
Neighbors I wrote for my f's & n's last April in Mendocino. It
all came together perfectly; and tho there's a lot of work and
changes yet to happen, the book is underway.

Carol and I got off briefly in Nashville, bought a tuna fish
sandwich, and returned to the plane just before takeoff. I went
to the bathroom to pee and noticed I needed a shave pretty bad.
My pants are torn and the zipper won't stay all the way up. Back
in the seat I ate my share of the sandwich and commented to
Carolanne on my state of disrepute. A man from the airlines came
over and asked us to get off. He wanted to talk with us. Para-
noia. Talk with us here, I said. He insisted. Okay, okay. He
asked us to take our stuff. We did. I said the plane was almost
ready to leave; would we be able to get back on? Yes. He turned
when we got in the terminal door and started a rap which suddenly
obviously was moving toward saying we'd been thrown off the
plane. At the request of pilot and stewardesses. No, not clothing,
offensive body odor! Needless to say, we did not stink. I has-
sled the man, threatened, cajoled but got nowhere. Meanwhile of
course the plane had taken off. There was never a chance to use
force, like rush back on or anything---once he got us to leave
we'd had it. Had I known what was coming I wouldn't have left.
But... they "refunded" the $7 Nashville to Memphis portion of our
tickets. I bought new ones from Southern Airways at $17 apiece--
a $20 burn. By turns I got furious, controlled myself, threatened
lawsuits, made appeals to courtesy and good public relations. But
there we were--$20 short, wretchedly offended, and two hours late
to Memphis, where Sue was waiting. Fury.
     And this forced me to think. My emotion was rage, my desire
destruction, revenge--not against the dude who took us off the
plane, not against the pilot but against American Airlines, the
corporate entity. But I realized--I couldn't avoid being aware of
it, I'm much too sane these days--that this was a blow of fate, a

fairly harmless taunt... I could act foolishly, throw things
or yell or (if my anger smouldered long enough) launch a lawsuit or public denunciation. But what would that do? Letting
off steam in a violent manner would entangle me further--
and a lawsuit would just be a money trip, and not worth the
time involved. Lawsuits & temper tantrums are foolish. And
I've already been cheerfully, without malice, writing stuff
that urges people to abandon the corporations, refuse to fly
or drive, etc---any action arising from today's incident would
be prideful...and useless. We mustn't nurture grievances if
we hope to be happy in the present. So I swallowed my pride
(well, I'm still working on it, we're in the air over Tennessee now) and admitted to myself that it's just what I should
expect if I place myself in the hands of the corporations,
                                        the old world.
It was my conscious decision to fly, both to the East in
the first place and now to the South, rather than spend more
time in travel--since cars and jets are equal evils, and you
submit yourself to an inorganic, neurotic environment either
way--and rather than just stay home. Why didn't I just stay
home? Uh...I don't know, home seems to be spread out, some-
how---but at any rate, having voluntarily, consciously gotten
into the situation it was my divine right and just dessert to
be smacked by it--I'm lucky it didn't kill me (yet) or stuff
me in jail. The Chicago 8, whose jury is still out, have suf-
fered already far more for participating in an unhealthy game
(politics) than any amount of hassle I might go thru with airlines.

And it's all the same thing--what's at issue is freedom.
And we <u>are free</u>---that's why I had to swallow my pride, that's
why I'm not on trial in Chicago. Because I didn't choose to
get involved in any game with the U.S.A. to the extent that I
would have to spend more of my life than I want (or can tolerate) hassling with the state. I went to the Pentagon march,
stayed and "fought" thru the night but avoided arrest, I took
part in the Plaza demonstration in New York etc etc. I occasionally in those days went to meetings at which plans for political action were discussed. But I found I had no taste for
meetings or plans, and eventually found I had no taste for "demonstrations"--'cause it's still just demonstrating, it's not
really doing it, "it" is living and you can't have it both ways
--you can show people how you live but you can't live to show
people stuff. Let there be no ambiguity here: my life comes
first, my writing comes out of my life and in harmony with it
or not at all.

So it was always apparent to me that protesting the state's
actions was tantamount to accepting the state's presence in one's
life, and that's an admission of defeat... the revolution is
now, there is no such thing as tomorrow. All "counterpolitics"
supports the system, the only thing to do with the system is a-
bandon it.

That's my feeling, anyway. And it's pretty much how I live.
I figure the only way I can _be_ free is to _assume_ I'm free, assume freedom and become master of my destiny. I'm certainly
as conscious as Richard Nixon, probably a lot more so, and
therefore it is _impossible_ for him to interfere willfully with
my life (accidentally, maybe--but that's not Richard or the
state, it's the cosmos). I am free because I choose to believe
I am--and I believe I have the strength to live up to my arrogance (and naiveté).

So you see I can't get _angry_ at American Airlines. It would
waste my time and energy, and why should I do that (because you
see it would be me doing it--_they_ can't touch me).

If I were to call up their president and tell him I thought
it was bad p.r. to treat people like niggers in 1970, especially
since the niggers are the dominant class, what would I be doing?
Giving my enemy good advice? What sense does that make? --I'd be
accepting the relationship with American Airlines that got me
in trouble in the first place, caught in a transition (I won't
accept their standards; they won't accept mine) I can get out
only by accepting American's world-system or **rejecting** it. Completely. I reject it, obviously, I'm a free man and I'm going to
stay **free, if** it occasionally costs me twenty bucks and a few
hours to relearn that (stay aware) the cost is cheap.

This all has to do with the medieval concept of freedom. But
my writing hand is tired.

...I suppose it will confuse a lot of my friends to hear me
say the Chicago 8 **are** responsible for where they are now---but
I have to say it, by my standards it would be an insult and
counter-revolutionary to suggest they are _not_ in control of
their fates. We are **ALL** in control of our fates and must be
ready to accept absolute responsibility for whatever is happening to us. The alternative is just to accept what's happening
to us, and that's not enough for me. Or to pretend to reject it...

Damn it, when will we see that defiance is no substitute
for freedom, **we are not actors**,
                                    we are gods

          and anyone who says he's not free
          to be what he wants to be
               is telling the truth.
                    Poor boob.

So if you think I'm insulting the Chicago 8, go back and read
what I said.
                I'm defending them.
Anyone who acts out his karmic role
            and accepts it and loves it
        is okay with me
Just do what you have to do
    you can't do better than that.
The Chicago 8 **are in** fact acting out extremely <u>important</u> roles
    ...if you're into aesthetics.
What I'm **saying is,** friends, don't
            you come crying to me
The   man who's put you where **you** are
        and the only one who **can** get you out
        or get you further
                is you.

The faster **we abandon,** the more we refuse to have anything to
do with, the old corrupt forms
                    the better off we'll be.
That's what I learned today.
Dishonest relationships are their own reward.

This is a book about people caught between the old world
and the new. Now in Arkansas, talking with Sue who works (thru
Vista) at a day-care center for black kids in a small town here,
I begin to realize just how hard it is...in many places one can
well wonder if a new world is even possible--it seems so far
away. And that feeling, combined with the unavoidable fact that
the old world is impossible, unbearable, can sometimes bring
despair.

This book is meant as an antidote to despair. I want you to
know it is possible to break through. I want to affirm our
strength, our potential--and I want to affirm all our perceptions
of just how bad the situation is, without harping on that, because if we pretend things aren't as bad, as difficult, as they
are, we'll never be able to see how good they are, how good they
can be. You may stick your head in the sand but despair will
still find you. But if you open your eyes, embrace all the pain
and joy, you will find--I know it, I have found it, I find it
again every day-- hope. And maybe more than hope: if you look
hard enough, see clear enough, you will discover a world more
beautiful than you can believe. You will find not despair, not
hope but conviction.
                And our faith will light the world.
                (things would be pretty dark without it)

In a few years young black citydwellers will start
moving to the country. They'll move to the South. And

they'll bring with them a strength, a conviction,
that will make this poor land shine. And the day-
care centers will become free schools, and a new
world, a world so far beyond anything that now
exists in America that few white Americans would
even dare dream of it, will begin to blossom.
   And you'll be a part of it, if you want to be.
If you dare to be.

Right now it seems we can't get off the ground.
It feels that way in Arkansas, anyway, and in
Kansas, and New York City. It feels that way in
San Francisco, to most of the people there. But
the free school in Mendocino is a charge of energy
that knocks me over, those kids are off the ground
and flying under their own power and the sky's no
limit. And I've seen it happening, and the conditions that led to breakthru, break away, are conditions that exist or are about to exist now every-
where---wherever there are children, wherever the
repression has peeled back far enough for kids to
see blue sky, it'll happen, kids'll get together and
run away with the world.

And those kids are our kids, but they're also <u>us</u>--
we can be as free as we want to be, as we dare to
be, right now! I know it, I feel it, tho without my
friends I might forget it fast enough,...
We all have to help each other, we have to help our
kids by not suppressing them...
   Hey! you parents--
   stop telling them what to do
   let 'em do what they want
        stop making all those judgments
             set 'em free!
 Don't intimidate them
        "for their own good"
   have some respect
   they are the strongest, surest, smartest people
   on the planet
   they're going to save the world
           don't get in their way
 if a kid wants to watch tv all the time
        that's what he wants to do
    if you don't like it, maybe
          you can seduce him away
        but if you order him away
             you're a pig
During the Hunger Show   Hugh Romney said to
the people watching: "Somebody get those kids'
parents to stop them from cutting holes in our
plastic thingy" and it was so counter-revolutionary
I wanted to scream.   kids must be set free
             talk to them yrself, Hugh

I'm getting carried away here
    there's so much to say
I want you to know we can break free,
        we are breaking free,
 of the chains that hold us down
     I want you to notice
                that what holds us to the chains
              is our own hands'
                 clinging
let go!
      just let yourself grow
   I want to tell you that if
        you think the world is doomed
               you're right
  there's nothing you can do to change it
               let it go

and discover there's a new world
                   all around you
  not doomed, not dying
      just being born
  climb aboard
              here we go...

And whenever you feel caught
        look at what you're caught between
it's always holding on   vs.
             pushing upward
 Vote for change
        vote with your life
life is change
        "security" is death warmed over
I want to tell you the truth
      I want to let you free

  sometimes it's so hard
          to see the other shore
that's when we need faith   to keep us going
there's no percentage in giving up
  and there's every reason for faith
  look at how far we've come!
  look at the fine work that's here for us to do

  this is a tract against suicide
    this is a tract against giving up

I can't tell you why
I can only help you look around
            look inside
   the truth is within you
     it's not in books
  it's in people's heads
     make love to your friends
       intuitive reality's the only one

I just can't say it clear enough
        you'll have to trust me
      there is reason to hope
      it's fun to make love
    this world will crumble but there's a
    fine world all around
        just beyond the walls
        beyond the old assumptions
Come wander with me in the wilderness
        don't be afraid
        I love you
    we can leave the world behind
            we'll build our own

Why wait any longer......?

this is the way the world begins...

Here in Arkansas it's become very clear to me
what's going to happen here and everywhere:
"communes"/extended families/whatever you call it will
start to happen, people will buy land in the country
and friends and acquaintances will drop by and stay to
live... here it'll be mainly black people, probably the
impetus will most often come from people who've been
in the cities, maybe were born there, and who know the
centers are falling apart, who've come to realize that
their small strength and certainty outweighs the
massive, intimidating bluff of the powers-that-be,
the governments, churches, corporations, bureaucracies
of every form, peopled by timid buck-passers pretending
it all adds up to certainty and power and not even aware
that it doesn't add up at all,
the city-dwellers who've seen the vaccuum
behind the veil of America and the-way-things-are
and believe in themselves instead,
the beautiful mad innocents who never knew or no longer
know that "you can't beat city hall"
will bring with them to the countryside energy and strength
and the courage to fulfill their visions, and they will find
that the land is still there,
the Ozark Mountains and Oregon coast and Oklahoma plains
and Minnesota wilderness, the vast unpopulated Canadian
wilds, they will find that one can live, here in
Arkansas you can easily grow your own food but there's no
tradition of "work the land" the tradition is "work for the
man who owns the land," work on the land for someone else
and so no honest open relationship exists,
people don't know that if you love your environment
and treat it well it will do the same for you. Ah, but
they'll learn, the time has come, and there'll be
black communes all over the South, hippie farms everywhere,
liberated proud sane people of every stripe will rediscover
the same natural laws, a way of life which feeds and is fed
by the environment (trees) and the environment (flesh).
Making love and all the varieties thereof (human interaction)
is the best fun there is, and it uses up nothing, no natural
resources. It even keeps you warm. And when the dying bureaucracies and old-world assumptions have crumbled enough,
people will start doing what they want to do, what they have
no choice but to do (intelligent blacks will have to leave
the cities and the business and politics world, just like
intelligent anyone), and then when the new world has got a
foothold--families/tribes/village-states ruled by consciousness law all over the landscape--and the old world has fallen
apart a bit more, the land will be seized, all that beautiful
land preserved by virtue of being "owned" by the government
and landholders and industry, for Future Use--there's plenty
of land in America, the U.S. and Canada (and Mexico and much
of the world), once the land is all in the hands of people

who are living in complete harmony (healthy relationships) with it--and then the children will go and reclaim
the cesspools, the cities and industrial areas, they'll
clean up the planet, it won't be hard 'cause they'll be
very strong   and very together
in ways we can't dream of now
and you'll see it all happen; in the next few years,
the next few days, the focus is shifting, balance is returning, the centers cannot hold, they are hemorrhaging...
organic forms, honest and open relationships, things that
can grow are the only things that will survive,
all else will rust and decay and clot and die...
the world begins now with a few Johnny Appleseeds, sowing
seeds of sanity in the fertile group consciousness,
functioning at high energy exciting their neighbors
seducing their friends to be equally high and feed back
the flow while the circles widen, it doesn't take much to
turn on a planet it just takes all you've got   and what
a pleasure it is to function at capacity: fullness: overload
and always a brother nearby to spill into, the families
keep growing towards total awareness
                    -may the circle be unbroken-
                            by and by...

and the news you read
      whether you read of strength like Manson's
                    in the newspapers
         or encounter a Valentine Smith
                    in some book
         or hear the strength of Mick Jagger
                singing "Live With Me"
                and it's news to you

is all just the story of a change in eras
myth of God emerging
      from a creature called man

it's happened before
we can only go further
don't get hung up in "history"
history only covers a small recent fraction
      of man's years on this planet
the last 2000 years   are a drop in the bucket
      if you want to draw a curve
            you'll have to go back farther

oh yes Man's becoming self-conscious again
      which means he's realizing a little bit more
            of his Godhood
      and suffering growing pains
      we want change but we fear it
      the news is: we cannot avoid it
         we may as well embrace it
                we'll enjoy it...

This book, <u>Time Between</u>, and its author's state of
mind may be characterized as the product of a conflict
(schizophrenia) in perception: discriminating vs.
indiscriminate.

The patient has made a lot of progress: he is no longer
in doubt as to which perceptions are "real," i.e, what
constitutes his "sane" state of mind (sanity, as Herbert
tells us, is the ability to swim). He is able, most of
the time, to embrace his "indiscriminate" point of view
and identify himself in terms of it; he is equally able,
as long as remains necessary, to discriminate in his perception of the external world, that which he has been
programmed to perceive via childhood training, newspapers,
advertising, cultural and man-made environmental influ-
ences. He will remain in a split-perception/schizophrenic
state as long as is necessary to his survival--i.e, until
his intuitive awareness is strong enough to incorporate
all external information into a sane world-system--
and it may be assumed that by the time the patient a-
chieves synonymity between intuitive assumptions and external events, the world will be a different place. Certainly it will no longer be possible for him to conceive
of an end to life-on-this-planet.

It should be noted that while the only thing that can
help the patient is his own inner strength (energy, clarity, imagination, perseverance) it will be possible, from
the external point of view, to measure his progress in
terms of the people around him. What we have here is a
classic case of the schizophrenic "messiah" mythos: a
conflict between an individual's perception and the gen-
erally agreed-on assumptions as to the nature of the collective world, which conflict is in ordinary times
resolved by the breakdown or successful adjustment of the
individual; in extraordinary times, usually on the cusp
of astrological eras, such conflict may be resolved, as
always, to the stronger party, who in this case may be
the individual---the external world, weakened by age,
collapses under the strain of conflict with a single individual, or series of "individuals," who embody the new
age, the new collective reality that is waiting in the
wings. Under these extraordinary circumstances, the schizophrenic actually progresses **through** all levels of madness
and reaches sanity, a new sanity so high above the old
that those persons who refuse to be crazy at all will almost certainly drown in the flood.

...It seems reasonable to assume that, at any given cusp,
there are innumerable persons who go through this schizophrenic messianic process; they collectively cause or

reflect--depending on your viewpoint--the world-change
called salvation.   The last cusp produced the myth of
Jesus Christ, perhaps one individual who attracted more
attention than most of the others who went thru similar
changes, perhaps a myth originally intentionally conceived to embody a process many individuals--many psyches--
went through. This present cusp seems not at all likely
to produce a similar myth; identification with a particular psyche and the changes it went through will not be
necessary this time around; this because unavoidably
the perception-change will climax in psychic unification.

So when the author of the present work achieves full
unambiguous sanity, you may rest assured we'll all know it.

In the meantime, enjoy the transition, folks!

                    -the end-
                 of Time Between

Books By Paul Williams

Practical philosophy:

Das Energi
Remember Your Essence
Fear of Truth (Energi Inscriptions)
Waking Up Together
The Book of Houses (with
    astrologer Robert Cole)
Coming
Nation of Lawyers
Common Sense
*How to Become Fabulously
    Wealthy at Home in
    30 Minutes*

Hippie memoirs:

Time Between
Apple Bay or Life on the Planet
Heart of Gold

Collections:

Pushing Upward
*Right to Pass and Other
    True Stories*

Music:

*Performing Artist, The Music of
    Bob Dylan,* Volumes I & II
*Brian Wilson & the Beach Boys —
    How Deep Is the Ocean?*
Neil Young — Love to Burn
*Rock and Roll: The 100
    Best Singles*
*Watching the River Flow:
    Observations on Bob Dylan's
    Art-in-Progress 1966-1995*
*The Map — Rediscovering
    Rock and Roll*
Outlaw Blues
Back to the Miracle Factory

Other arts:

The 20th Century's Greatest Hits
*Only Apparently Real: The World
    of Philip K. Dick*

Edited by Paul Williams:

*The International Bill of
    Human Rights*
*The Complete Stories of Theodore
    Sturgeon*
(magazines: *Crawdaddy!*
The PKD Society Newsletter)

ALL IN PRINT. For a catalog or ordering information, contact:
Entwhistle Books, Box 232517 Encinitas CA 92023 USA
www.cdaddy.com (look for **ENTWHISTLE BOOKS** button)
phone or fax: 760-753-1815   email: EB@cdaddy.com